ESCAPE TO ː ʀ!

Impressions of walkiː

By Michael Hedges

FOREST PUBLISHING

First published in 1997 by FOREST PUBLISHING, Woodstock, Liverton, Newton Abbot, Devon TQ12 6JJ

Copyright   © Michael R. Hedges 1997

British Library Cataloguing in Publication Data

A catalogue record for this book is available from the British Library.

ISBN 0–9527297–2–5

Forest Publishing

Editorial, design and layout by:
Mike Lang

Typeset by:
Carnaby Typesetting, Torquay, Devon TQ1 1EG

Printed and bound in Great Britain by:
BPC Wheatons Ltd., Exeter, Devon EX2 8RP

Cover photographs:

Front – The view westwards to Sharp Tor from among the rock-stacks of Fur Tor on northern Dartmoor.

Back – The main rock-pile of Fur Tor.

CONTENTS

		Page
	Introduction	5
1	Fox Tor Mire	15
2	Fur Tor	24
3	Tavy Cleave	29
4	Red Lake	36
5	Erme Pits	45
6	The East Dart Valley	56
7	Bleak House	63
8	Aune Head Mire	70
9	Lints Tor	77
10	Cranmere Pool	85
11	Beardown Man	93
12	Watern Tor	100
13	The Whitebarrows	107
14	A Walk on the Wild Side	116
15	Great Kneeset	123
16	Soggy, Boggy and Foggy	130
17	Whitehorse Hill	135
18	Dartmoor North and South	146
	Bibliography	151
	Index	154
	The Author	160

ACKNOWLEDGEMENTS

The preparation of this book has required many physically active hours of walking across Dartmoor, especially as many locations had to be re-visited in order that suitable photographs could be taken. I have also had to spend a lot of mentally active time hunched either over a steering-wheel or a word-processor. All this was made possible by the patience and tolerance of my family, to whom I owe a large debt of thanks. In particular, they made the task much easier and more fulfilling by accompanying me on many of the walks.

By coincidence, although I live 175 miles from Dartmoor, I have an immediate neighbour, Derek Giles, who, like myself, is an ardent Dartmoor enthusiast. I am grateful to him for his verbal encouragement (often blunt!), his comments on the manuscript and for permission to use some of his photographs, which are acknowledged individually. The remaining photographs, including those used for the cover illustrations, are from my own collection.

I am grateful to have been able to use in chapter 1 verbatim extracts from that inspirational masterpiece *The Hound of the Baskervilles* by Sir Arthur Conan Doyle. These extracts are copyright © Sheldon Reynolds, 1996 and are reproduced by kind permission of Jonathan Clowes Ltd., London, on behalf of Sheldon Reynolds.

Listed in the Bibliography are a number of books and periodicals related to Dartmoor that I have been able to use as a source of reference and for which, in each instance, I acknowledge with thanks the work of the author concerned.

Last, but not least, I should like to thank Hilary Walker for reading and commenting on the manuscript in its early stages.

❋❋❋❋❋

DEDICATION

This book is dedicated to my family.

❋❋❋❋❋

INTRODUCTION

Why escape? Why Dartmoor? I'll try to explain. In the middle of the moor, at Princetown, is a great prison, built of old moorstone and equipped with modern security devices. On an overcast day the sight of this grim edifice evokes feelings every bit in keeping with those aroused by the surrounding moorland. To any of its inmates the thought that anyone should want to escape to Dartmoor, as opposed to from it, must seem crazy indeed! Yet escaping to Dartmoor is, for me, an act of renewal, of revitalisation, of rekindling enthusiasm for life's daily grind. What am I escaping from? Simply the pressure, responsibility and routine which go hand in hand with the reassuring security of home and working life. In the late 20th century, life is hectic, crowded and demanding. Everyone needs to be able to step off the treadmill from time to time, to recharge batteries and to find space. The way I choose to do this is to walk in the wilderness of Dartmoor.

It is not, however, that Dartmoor is on my doorstep; I grew up, and still live, on the chalk downlands of mid-Hampshire. Surely the countryside there can offer some freedom and open space? Well, I do not think that it can any longer. When I was a boy the local countryside seemed vast and mysterious. What was over that hill? Where did that path lead? To an adult, though, this same countryside now seems tame and regimented by agriculture. I now know what is on the other side of the hill and where that path leads. Houses, roads and civilisation have encroached too far with the result that the feeling of being in the unknown has vanished forever.

The need to recapture that sense of the unknown is, for me, so strong that I am prepared to, and often do, drive the 350-mile round trip to Dartmoor in order to walk over its remotest parts, returning the same day: its unique landscape offers so much. The countryside of south-west England still has that untouched quality about it that Hampshire possessed back in the early 1960s. But Dartmoor is a world apart, even from its close surroundings – just a short distance over the hills from the roads which skirt the moor is a primeval landscape, miraculously preserved from human interference and desecration. Mile upon mile of high, empty grassland rolls away to the far horizon, punctuated by young river valleys and stark, prominent tors. The emptiness and, yes, sometimes the bleakness of the place captivates my imagination whenever I walk there. The cares and worries of daily life are swept away like so many inconsequentials. Here, there is preserved a landscape hardly changed from that which our primitive ancestors gazed across 10,000 years ago. Its vastness is such that it would take a whole lifetime of exploration for one to become fully familiar with the topography. Furthermore, apart from the appearance of the hills and valleys, there is an infinite sub-set of impressions of Dartmoor. These are the variations in the weather, light and season, and are as important a part of the Dartmoor experience as the shape of the moorland itself.

No doubt mid-Wales, Northumberland, Cumbria and the Scottish Highlands are equally, if not more, vast and wild. But, for anyone who has walked in its innermost parts, Dartmoor's special quality is that it strikes one as a place from which civilisation has receded, rather than one which is threatened by its advance. For all over the wilderness of the high moor there remain the signs left by human beings in their futile attempts to live and work on it. These range from prehistoric hut circles and standing stones to old tin mines and abandoned china clay workings, and, whilst some are ancient and some not so ancient, they all add interest to the landscape and provide a wealth of material for the academic or the specialist.

My wife and I began to explore Dartmoor before our three boys appeared on the scene, but after they were born we were not able to do so for some time. Even with the best child-carriers, two people cannot carry three small children on long walks! But even when they were still quite young, we began to introduce them to walking by taking them out on to the Hampshire Downs. This was the first time that I had done any local rural walking since my early boyhood – teenage interests had soon obscured the simple pleasures of discovering wildlife in its natural habitat. But it was in this renewed acquaintance with the Hampshire countryside that I realised it could no longer offer the sense of complete freedom which it had once given me. My thoughts, therefore, turned once again to Dartmoor. One August, when we considered that our boys now had enough strength (we became convinced of this after they walked up Snowdon without a single complaint!), we arranged a week's holiday on the moor. Once there, I quickly realised that on Dartmoor the qualities now gone from rural Hampshire were still to be found, and in far greater measure. Here, at last, we had found a place where there was a sense of complete detachment from the frenetic pace of an overcrowded modern world.

The only problem remaining was how to get to Dartmoor regularly. Until then it had been a distant destination for an annual holiday. But three months later I set off to the moor very early one frosty Saturday morning in late November. Arriving at Whiteworks, near Princetown, at about 8.30 a.m., I walked out to Erme Pits and back, eventually returning home at 7.30 that same evening. After that, Sunday was strictly reserved for a lie-in (and recovery!), but from that day I knew that regular visits to the moor were no longer a pipe-dream. And so, I now invite you to share my experiences of walking in the most remote parts of Dartmoor, although I would caution that the routes described are those which I happen to have followed; they are not always the easiest that I could have taken – as I often discovered afterwards! I would add that I do not attempt to describe in detail every single feature of interest on the walks as I don't pretend to have any expertise or specialist knowledge of Dartmoor objects such as boundary stones, kistvaens and so on (there are many excellent books on these subjects, some of which are listed in the Bibliography). Rather, I want to convey the uplifting feelings that I have experienced and to share the impressions that I have gained from walking on the moor. At the same time, however, I will not ignore the more interesting and surprising things to be seen there and, every so often, I'll throw in a few personal views with which you are welcome to disagree.

Finally, some words of warning; should you venture out on to the moor you will find that to experience the solitude of this unique place requires a certain amount of resilience. It also presents a degree of risk, especially if you are not properly prepared, and it is for these reasons that I have set out below some advice on the hazards likely to be encountered, what to wear and what to take:–

The Hazards

The primary source of danger to the Dartmoor walker is the use by the army of the three firing ranges – Okehampton, Willsworthy and Merrivale – on the northern moor. Live firing takes place regularly throughout the year with the exception of certain periods, such as the month of August.

There are many walks in this book which either enter or pass very close to one or more of the firing ranges. These are the walks to Fur Tor, Tavy Cleave, Bleak House, Cranmere Pool, East Dart Valley, Lints Tor, Watern Tor, Beardown Man, Okement Hill, Great Kneeset, Whitehorse Hill and Hound Tor.

For information on firing times, a 24-hour recorded telephone message is available on the following numbers:-

Paignton   (01803) 559782
Exeter   (01392) 270164
Plymouth   (01752) 501478
Okehampton   (01837) 52939

(It gives the week's live firing times for each of the Dartmoor ranges, and for the Tregantle range near Torpoint in Cornwall).

When live firing is in progress the ranges are out of bounds to the public. At such times, red warning flags fly on all the major high points around the range boundaries and look-outs are posted at key points to watch for stray walkers. The range boundaries, themselves, are marked by posts with alternating red and white horizontal bands, added to which there are signs which warn walkers when they are approaching a firing range and caution them not to touch any metal objects that might be found.

Anyone planning a walk in the northern wilderness should obviously check the firing times first. Otherwise they face a wasted journey or, at best, a switch to an unplanned walk on an unaffected part of the moor.

Even when the ranges are accessible to walkers, one frequently comes across the remains of bullets, mortars or flares. Usually these have been fired but, as a precaution, they should always be left well alone. Live mortars are particularly dangerous and these, sometimes even of World War II vintage, are still found. This is in spite of extensive clearing-up operations that have been carried out by the army over the intervening years. The danger, in fact, was illustrated only too well in June 1995 when a family with three children from Ashburton were letterboxing on Great Mis Tor. One of them found a live mortar, dating from 1942, picked it up and threw it. The mortar exploded, causing shrapnel injuries to all three children. Thankfully these injuries, although serious for one child, were not fatal. Live mortars, or indeed any metal object, should not be touched, but reported to the police or military authorities.

Another danger on the moor is getting lost, and I'm not only talking about times when the legendary Dartmoor mists come down. Once you are up on the high, central plateau of the northern or southern wilderness the landscape can be very featureless. Even on a clear day, anyone unfamiliar with the moor will need at some time to confirm their direction with a compass and a 1:25,000 scale Ordnance Survey walker's map of Dartmoor. If these are not carried the consequences could be serious in winter or in bad weather. At best, poor navigation may result in a very long walk to one's original destination.

If you do become lost and cannot find your path the traditional remedy is to find a stream and follow it downhill. You may well end up miles away from your intended route, but at least you will have left the moor safely behind rather than run the risk of merely walking around in a circle and becoming exhausted. I should emphasise that this old adage works on Dartmoor, but could, of course, be fraught with danger in mountainous areas!

If I am walking on the moor alone, I always leave a note of my route at home with my family – and I stick to that route. This is good practice, even if you are accompanied. There is always a risk of becoming stranded due to a twisted or broken ankle, and it is no use relying on other people coming past as more often than not you will see no-one else near at hand, if at all. I also always carry a whistle with me as a means of attracting attention in the event of injury. This is because I could still end up a quarter of a mile or more either side of the path between the places on my route, even if I have stayed on my notified route, and someone might have to try to find me.

The other fundamental point to make about moorland walking is that you can make things easier for yourself if you try to go on to the moor when the weather forecast is good. That, however, is easier said than done because weather forecasting for Dartmoor is not particularly reliable. For example, I have been on the high moor in rain when the weather at the lower levels of Devon is fine, and vice versa. Nevertheless, bearing in mind that I have to travel 175 miles to get to Dartmoor, I tend not to go unless I'm fairly confident that the weather is going to be dry. Not many people in their right minds will start a walk on the moor in pouring rain as there really is very little pleasure to be gained from walking in such conditions. I walk on Dartmoor for inspiration and to escape from life's routine; but, if it's wet there, I'd rather stay at home, thank you!

I find that the weather forecasts broadcast on any radio station are fairly useless most of the time, unless there really is no doubt that unbroken sunshine or rain is on its way. Televised forecasts are better, but only in any way reliable for Dartmoor for a maximum of one day ahead. Even then, the forecasters are up against the variations in local climate, and on a national forecast they aren't usually too bothered about such details. Then there are the telephone forecasts for Devon and Cornwall. These are generally good and do tend to distinguish between the moors and the lower ground, but it takes at least an expensive minute before you get the information you really want – after the forecast has been padded out with air quality, mean sea-level pressure at Plymouth and so on. I only wish they were updated more frequently; it is frustrating listening to a forecast for a part of the day which is already over!

Despite the dangerous qualities attributed to Dartmoor bogs by writers such as Sir Arthur Conan Doyle, these have really been over-dramatised. You could certainly get very wet feet and legs if you persisted in trying to walk across Fox Tor Mire or Broad Marsh, but it is very unlikely that you would come to any real harm. Compared to the mires, I think there is more danger in walking across clitter or rocks strewn around the tors. It is so easy to lose your balance and stumble, risking a broken or sprained ankle, or worse.

Some of the old tin mines on the moor can present a risk. The shafts have long been filled in, or fenced, but some of the mines have one or more deep gashes into the nearby hillside; these are all that remain of worked-out veins of mineral. If you happen to be walking on such a hillside, you could be very seriously injured, or even killed, if you fell down into one of them. A typical example is at the old Wheal Katherine Mine on the south-eastern slopes of Eylesbarrow, near Plym Ford.

Adders are plentiful on the moor and are active in the warmer seasons. They will only attack if cornered; otherwise they will probably want to get away from you as quickly as you will from them. But if you do get bitten, you should get off the moor as quickly as possible for medical treatment because adder bites can sometimes be fatal if not treated quickly.

The next hazards to mention are those of being dressed unsuitably and being ill-equipped for the adverse weather which you may well encounter.

Snake charming is not advisable! An adder is held at bay by a walking stick.

Derek Giles

What to Wear

There are umpteen sources of information and guidance on what to wear when walking on the moor. If you so wished, you could spend a small fortune on clothing and footwear, but I don't think that this is at all necessary for Dartmoor, especially if you give yourself a chance of walking in comfort by choosing a day when the weather is likely to be suitable. Obviously, if you do go out on to the moor in Arctic cold, or when it is atrociously wet, then you will need to invest in equipment and clothing which is up to dealing with such conditions and the risks that go with them. My advice, however, is going to be restricted to what is suitable for reasonable walking conditions, but will give sufficient protection if the weather should change suddenly for the worse.

First of all, footwear, which I would stress must provide good ankle support. In my opinion, for most times of the year, a good pair of wellington boots with moulded studded soles is the best all-round footwear for moorland walking. This statement, I accept, may upset the mountaineering purists, and in places like the Welsh mountains I readily admit that I would not dream of wearing wellingtons because they are highly unsuited to walking over wet rocks and are a greater weight to carry upwards on the ends of one's legs! Dartmoor, however, is not mountainous. Rather, the prevailing condition encountered is that of ground which is very wet underfoot and then even the most expensive pair of walking boots is of little use if you sink more than six or seven inches into waterlogged ground. Only in the hot, dry conditions that can sometimes occur in the height of summer would I concede that walking boots are a better proposition: they are cooler and, if you do get a wet foot, the heat of the day will soon reduce the discomfort. In fact, I do keep a cheap (£35 in 1994) pair of walking boots, with leather uppers and composite soles, for such circumstances, but even then there is another potential problem inasmuch that should they become wet it takes a long time to dry them if the leather is not to be damaged. This is particularly troublesome if you are taking a week's walking holiday, for should you get your walking boots wet, they won't be dry by the next day, so you will need at least one spare pair. In contrast, wellington boots can be dried out very quickly if they get wet inside. Once, for example, when we were staying at Mary Tavy, I got my wellingtons wet inside whilst walking in the Huntingdon Warren area. We then drove back to Mary Tavy with my wet wellies in the front passenger's floor-well of the car. The heater and fan were on full blast and directed to the floor only, with all the car windows open. By the time that we had reached Mary Tavy, three-quarters of an hour later, my wellingtons had dried out completely and were almost too hot to touch!

As important as the boots, themselves, is what you wear inside them. No matter how hot it is, and whether I'm wearing wellingtons or walking boots, I always wear one pair of short, everyday socks underneath a second pair of thick woollen walking socks. I once made the mistake of wearing two pairs of thin socks because the day was hot. My walk started from Harford Moor Gate and went up the track-bed of the Red Lake Tramway into the upper Erme Valley, and over the Plym Valley to Eylesbarrow and Nun's Cross Farm. The last stage went down to Burrator Reservoir, over into the Walkham Valley and finished at our holiday cottage in Horrabridge. At the end of this 15-mile walk my feet were in a murderous state. I had a large blister on each heel, due entirely to the poor protection given by the thin socks which I had worn. There was also a smaller blister under each big toe. I had learnt the hard way that, no matter how hot it might be, one's feet must be properly protected from the pounding they will get on a long walk. Even with thick walking socks, the heels tend to wear thin quite quickly and they should then be discarded.

Moving upwards, I make a point of not wearing shorts on the moor, even in hot weather, because of the risk of unnecessary insect bites and sheep tics. The latter are grey-brown, up to 5 millimetres long and inhabit bracken and tall grass at warmer times of the year. If a bare leg comes wading through the grass they attach themselves gratefully to it, bite into it and feed on its blood, sometimes causing infections. There are also some wicked horse-flies on Dartmoor, capable of nasty bites, and they tend to go for bare forearms. There is usually time to flick them off before they get stuck in!

Most types of casual trousers are suitable for walking as long as they are reasonably comfortable and strong. I always carry with me a pair of waterproof leggings rolled up in my backpack. They are superb for keeping out not only driving rain but also the cold wind.

And so to the jacket. In summer or winter I wear a shirt and jumper under my jacket. In summer that jacket will be a waterproof kagoule with a hood, which I roll up into my backpack if it is hot. But I have yet to find a kagoule capable of keeping out Dartmoor rain. Between you and me, I tend to sweat rather a lot and I often end up damp on the inside, whether from rain or sweat. In winter I wear my one expensive item, a Barbour thornproof wax jacket. These are excellent and long-lasting, with several large inside pockets which take some time to discover in their entire number! Hoods are available to snap on to the jacket; but I usually wear a flat cap if it is cold – it is amazing how much heat is lost through the head. I think it is better not to wear bright colours on the moor, because they look a bit incongruous. Against that, they show up better if you are stranded and rescuers are looking for you. A scarf is very effective in helping to keep out a biting wind, and I always carry, or wear, a pair of woollen gloves in cold weather. Finally, I have to confess that, on occasions, I have even taken a small foldaway umbrella with me in the backpack if there is a risk of driving rain. If the weather turns lousy I am quite prepared to sacrifice some ego and dignity by putting up an umbrella to keep dry on Dartmoor. It can be very effective in a short squally shower, always provided that it does not blow inside out!

In spring or autumn I always find it difficult to judge whether to wear my Barbour or kagoule. Often it can feel cold when you step out of the car to start walking, but after a mile or so you will have warmed up considerably. If the sun comes out and it gets hot then the Barbour has to come off, but it is then very awkward to carry.

What to Take

I never walk on Dartmoor without a map, a compass and a backpack with other essentials in it. As far as the map is concerned, both the old one inch to one mile (1:63,360) and the newer 1:50,000 Landranger maps are too small a scale for walking. They are insufficiently detailed; for example, they do not show the newtake walls on Dartmoor and these can be very important landmarks if you are lost. They also give the impression that distances are smaller than they really are. The best one to use is the O.S. 1:25,000 walker's map of the moor. This is a double-sided map which covers nearly the whole of the National Park, certainly all the areas of good moorland walking. It is, however, rather large and cumbersome, and I find that the best way to carry it is in a waterproof map holder slung around your neck, with the map folded inside so as to cover the whole area of the walk. Otherwise it is surprising how quickly a map exposed to rain assumes the texture and consistency of porridge! A map holder with an adjustable neck cord can be bought from any good camping shop. An alternative to all this is a map encapsulated in clear plastic, but these are rather cumbersome and do not fold up to a very compact size.

Next, compasses. I should say from the outset that a small button compass is useless. I carry two compasses with me. The first has a rotating scale and a transparent perspex base marked with a direction arrow and various distance scales around its perimeter. It has a neck cord, which makes it secure and easier to use in bad weather: the rotating scale allows the user to take and set bearings. My second compass is a sighting compass, which, with its mirror and cross-wire, enables a set bearing to be followed very accurately when walking. Again, a good camping shop will stock a selection of both types of compass.

As I mentioned earlier, I always take with me a whistle to attract attention should I become immobilised by a twisted or broken ankle. A torch could also be very useful if you happen to run out of daylight on the moor.

I recently switched from a 19-litre backpack to one of 35-litre capacity. This was not because I necessarily wanted to carry a lot more equipment. It was just that I often found that the straps of the smaller backpack had to be stretched quite tightly to fasten them with all my gear inside. This gradually resulted in the stitching giving way strand by strand. The larger backpack avoids this problem; it also has a waist strap, like a child-carrier, and this relieves the back and shoulders of some of the load.

The backpack must be of sufficient size to hold a number of essential items. Principal among these is, of course, food and drink. If I am walking with my family, we spread the load amongst our backpacks and carry with us a thermos flask, cups, a small plastic bottle of milk, coffee, cartons and bottles of fruit juice and other cold drinks, in addition to sandwiches, crisps, chocolate biscuits and fruit in plastic ice cream containers with lids. If I am walking alone, I tend to dispense with the thermos on the grounds of its size and weight, and carry cold drinks only, along with the food. It depends really on personal preference and how much weight you are prepared to carry. The thing to do is to have with you more food and drink than you are likely to need for an uneventful walk (by uneventful, I mean that you get to your destination without mishap!). This will allow for some stand-by supplies in case you get lost, or cold, or both. In particular, on a hot day the temptation to use up too much drink too early in the walk must be resisted.

Other items in my backpack are a pair of waterproof leggings, a first-aid kit and a tube of antiseptic cream. If space permits, I take a camera and a small pair of binoculars. Generally, I leave behind in the car a change of socks, trousers, shirt and pullover. After a long walk, even if you have kept dry, you will feel much better driving home in a pair of clean socks and a clean shirt. If you are undertaking an exceptionally long walk it would be advisable to carry these spare clothes with you.

I have tried one or two pedometers, but with limited success. The vigorous, varied-stride walking over Dartmoor country does not seem suitable for them. I lost one, which became unclipped from my belt. The second one that I tried appeared to be fairly accurate for the first 6 miles, but half an hour later it read 13 miles! They seem very expensive for what they are, and I can usually manage a reasonable estimate of the distance I have walked by scaling roughly in kilometres, using the map squares, and then converting to miles.

The very last item I will mention is a good walking stick. I always use one. It is invaluable in helping you to keep your balance over rocky ground and through boggy areas. You can also use it to transmit arm power to the ground in order to help you up a particularly steep hillside.

So there we are. You don't need a Himalayan survival kit, particularly if you use common-sense and judgement in choosing the days when to walk and when not to walk on the moor. Some of what you take and wear is purely down to personal choice. But always be prepared for bad weather – quite often your preparations will be justified!

Michael Hedges
January 1997

✳✳✳✳✳

1

FOX TOR MIRE

My first images of Dartmoor came to me when I was about 10 years old, not from a holiday visit, but through the pages of Sir Arthur Conan Doyle's classic, *The Hound of the Baskervilles*. The book paints a vivid portrait of the moor as a place of seemingly infinite extent, solitude and menace. An apparently supernatural hound from hell emerges into reality from an old family legend to frighten one of the last of the Baskervilles into an early grave. The story made a deep impression on me and was the cause of many a nightmare, but, like a mouse mesmerised by a snake, I could not resist reading and re-reading it.

Just as I thought I was overcoming the fear induced in me by the story, along came a televised version. The producer had added a few sinister effects of his own, such as a Baskerville family motto, 'Cave canem nocte', which, as my schoolboy Latin told me all too well, means 'Beware the dog by night'. Inexplicably, these subtle, yet rather trifling, embellishments triggered a return of those bad dreams but, at the same time, I could not bring myself to miss a single episode.

Conan Doyle's tale tantalises the reader who attempts to pinpoint the supposed location of Baskerville Hall on Dartmoor. Real place names like Merripit, Bellever, Vixen Tor, Fernworthy and Black Tor, all within six or seven miles of Princetown, are mentioned as the story unfolds, interspersed with the fictitious Coombe Tracey, Foulmire and Lafter Hall. Just as you think, after some time poring over a map, that you have finally found a location which fits well with the narrative, you suddenly remember Sherlock Holmes telling Watson in chapter 3 about the environs of Baskerville Hall – 'fourteen miles away, the great convict prison of Princetown'. Collapse of theory!

Such contradictions have not prevented Holmes aficionados from indulging in endless debate about the setting of the book. This debate, of course, takes no account of the artistic licence which Conan Doyle was entitled to pursue in creating the setting for his story. However, one of the few points of consensus which have emerged is that the Great Grimpen Mire, into which the villain finally flounders to a slimy end, was inspired by Conan Doyle's visit to Fox Tor Mire.

Fox Tor Mire can be approached very easily. A narrow metalled road, beset by stone walls, extends tentatively from Princetown into the depths of the southern moor. As if its courage has finally deserted it, it ends at the site of the Whiteworks Tin Mine, on the edge of the mire. Driving out of Princetown, this road feels hemmed in, on one side by belts of conifer trees and on the other by the ground rising westwards to South Hessary Tor. But, quite suddenly, these shrouds fall away; the trees are left behind, the road drops to the left and the mire is revealed below, a vast natural amphitheatre stretching away for half a mile before the ground rises again towards Fox Tor and Crane Hill.

Leaving the car in the old quarry where the Devonport Leat flows under the road, it is worth just pausing by the roadside to accustom the senses to what lies before. Of sound, there is very little; certainly no baying hound, only the trill of a skylark or the muffled calls of sheep and cattle scattered here and there among the rocks on the nearby hillside. As if in compensation, the eyes strain to assimilate the intricate amalgam of scale, form and subtle colour which appears on all sides. To the right, the Devonport Leat winds along the hillside and disappears from view. Opposite, the slight undulations of Hand Hill, Fox Tor, Crane Hill and Caters Beam rise to meet the canopy of sky. Further to the left, the slopes of Ter Hill drop down to the narrow valley through which the River Swincombe carries away any water which the green-brown spongy mire is unable to retain.

Our walk takes us around the rim of the mire, never more than half a mile from its edge. Leaving the quarry, we follow the Devonport Leat in a south-westerly direction along the slopes of Nun's Cross Hill. Rounding the shoulder of the hill, we may disturb a heron from its pre-tensioned poise in the leat, awaiting a shoal of the tiny brown trout, which are often to be seen in the shallow water. As the leat swings away from the mire, we continue along the bankside path and eventually reach the gated portal of a small tunnel, into which the leat disappears. This is Nun's Cross Tunnel, which, along with the Meavy Aqueduct 2 1/2 miles to the west, is a tribute to the engineering skill and sheer hard labour that created the Devonport Leat between the years 1793 and 1797.

The leat was conceived to supply water to the growing naval establishment at Devonport, where the first dock had been completed in 1695. It draws its water from weirs on the rivers Cowsic and West Dart, and also the Blackbrook, and generally follows an ingenious, gradually descending route along the contours. But every so often, where the topography makes this impossible, there are aqueducts and this tunnel. Nowadays, the leat is curtailed, discharging its peaty, yellow water into Burrator Reservoir, near Sheepstor. Here it is stored, along with the waters of the Meavy, Newleycombe Lake, Narrator Brook and Sheepstor Brook, forming one of several sources of water supply for the Plymouth area.

The Devonport Leat as it re-appears from the west portal of Nun's Cross Tunnel.

Nun's Cross Tunnel is some 648 yards long. It carries the leat under the watershed of the Rivers Meavy and Swincombe, a shoulder of land straddled by Nun's Cross Farm, which can now be seen a short way ahead. As we walk around the drystone wall of the farm enclosure, we see, on the west side, Nun's Cross, itself, standing sentinel by the path

Nun's (or Siward's) Cross, with the farm beyond. Note the repair and also the inscription 'Boc Lond'.

17

known as the Abbots' Way. Not only is it one of the tallest stone crosses on Dartmoor, standing about 7 feet high, but it is also very ancient; we know from the records of the 1240 Perambulation of the Forest of Dartmoor that it existed then and formed, as it still does, one of the boundary points of the Forest. It is also known as Siward's Cross, reputedly after one of the Earls of Northumberland, who owned large areas of Devon in Saxon times. The indistinct inscription 'Syward', which could possibly be 'Siward', is carved on the eastern face of the cross.

To the east of the cross is the Forest of Dartmoor, while to the west is the manor of Walkhampton, which was at one time owned by Buckland Abbey. It is believed that evidence of this lies in the words 'Boc Lond', which are carved on the western face of the cross and are clearly legible when the sun is suitably placed. In the 1840s the shaft of the cross was broken, and one can still see the iron strap used to effect the repair as well as the fracture itself.

Walking past Nun's Cross Farm on the way out to the heart of the southern moor, I always feel a thrill at what is yet to come. Anyone seeking to reach Eylesbarrow, Plym Head, Ducks Pool or Erme Pits from Whiteworks will find themselves passing this lonely spot. For centuries here, the cross was the only tangible sign of man. Then came the leat and the tin mines, followed, in 1870, by the building of the farm in an ultimately vain attempt to eke a living from these hostile surroundings. Now empty, except for occasional use as an outdoor training centre, the farm stands silent, a stone memorial to a venture that was surely doomed from the outset. For me, the empty farm is a signpost that I am passing a place at the limit of civilisation's reach and am about to enter the real wilderness.

Nun's Cross Farm.

Today, however, we will resist the temptation to strike out southwards and, instead, we must head towards Fox Tor Mire. East of the farm, we can follow the Abbots' Way across Nun's Cross Brook. Then, rather than climbing the slope to the top of Hand Hill, we turn eastwards, over Whealam Stream and proceed among the scattered rocks of the drier land known as Sand Parks, which rises from the southern edge of the mire. Hard by our route we see Goldsmith's Cross, a once-fallen medieval marker that was discovered and re-erected in 1903 by Lieutenant Malcolm (later Vice-Admiral Sir Malcolm) Goldsmith.

A quarter of a mile or so further on is another cross, this time set in a collection of granite slabs. This monument is called Childe's Tomb, and the legend behind it is that a Cild (precursor of Childe), or Saxon lord, became separated from his hunting party in atrocious weather on the moor. With no shelter nearby, he killed his horse, disembowelled it and protected himself from the cold inside its carcass. Despite this, he froze to death, but not before he had written his will in blood, leaving his Plymstock estate to whichever church should happen to bury him. Monks from Tavistock found the body and, while conveying it back to their abbey for burial, had to build a new bridge across the Tavy to avoid losing the body to rivals keen to bury it and gain the estate for themselves.

I have recounted this legend for completeness only. I am afraid that I simply cannot take the story of Childe's Tomb at all seriously: Dartmoor, perhaps understandably for a place of such extremes, has regrettably more than its fair share of implausible legends, of which this is one.

Childe's Tomb – a meaningless monument!

I know that some academic research has uncovered a story with apparently good credentials on which the legend may be based. But the embellishments – oh dear! The disembowelling of a horse to shelter in its carcass; worse still, the instant erection by monks of a bridge to ensure that the burial of the body took place at Tavistock and that they inherited the estate!

The 'tomb', itself, probably dates from much later than the story forming the basis of the legend. The cross was added later still. There is no indication that the supposed event took place anywhere near here, and there is probably no-one buried underneath it. To my mind, a monument such as Nun's Cross, which is known to be of great age and is authentically documented as marking an ancient boundary, merits far more respect and worth than this imposter. The legend of Childe's Tomb is only capped for sheer nonsense by that of Cranmere Benjy, on which I shall waste no space, except to say that it can be read in many other books about Dartmoor!

Fox Tor Mire, looking eastwards.

Moving swiftly on, we take the higher ground above Childe's Tomb, heading for Fox Tor, which, from a distance, does not proclaim itself as a significant vantage point. It is only when the quite steep, but short, ascent of its slopes has been made that one can appreciate the panoramic prospect which it offers. Then, when resting on one of its outcrops, with the afternoon sun behind, the eye is first drawn to the cloud shadows moving across the green slopes of the distant hills to the north. Much nearer to hand is the huge, natural bowl of the mire. For a moment, one can imagine two great armies sweeping down the slopes and across this plain towards each other at the start of some epic battle.

But there are very few human activities which Dartmoor is prepared to tolerate and, remembering the sheer physical impossibility of such an event happening on this terrain, one is quickly jolted back to reality. Meanwhile, behind this grandstand seat, the ground continues to rise southwards, eventually levelling out to form the watershed between the Rivers Erme and Swincombe. Yet further south lies the centre of the southern moor, not on our route today, but a place which must be visited if one is to experience the ultimate sense of solitude which the moor can provide.

It is time to descend the hill to make an easy crossing of the streams which flow into the mire at its south-east corner. Long ago the tin miners dug a deep trench known as Fox Tor Gert into the hill; out of this a small stream flows to join the infant waters of the River Swincombe as it tumbles down the natural funnel formed by the soggy slopes of Ter Hill and Nakers Hill. Making our way as best we can across the streams, using the slippery, rounded rocks as stepping stones, we can strike the lower part of Ter Hill and head for the obvious ruins of Fox Tor Farm: this was built in 1812 and, until it ceased to be occupied in 1863, was the base for a succession of individuals, and families, who tried with varying degrees of perseverance to wring some form of agricultural profit from the exposed surroundings.

Gateway in newtake wall, with Fox Tor beyond.

We now walk north-westwards over the low shoulder of Ter Hill and continue until the ground begins to drop steeply into the narrow valley of the Swincombe, where the water collected by the mire is offered the only means of escape. Above the river, on our side, is a prominent dry channel, which is all that remains of the Wheal Emma Leat. Built in the last century to augment the waters of the River Mardle so as to provide a more efficient driving force for the machinery of the Mardle Valley Tin Mine, this leat twisted along the contours from Fox Tor Mire for about 8 miles to join the River Mardle above Chalk Ford.

It is not always easy to cross the River Swincombe at the point that we have now reached. In autumn and winter it is fast flowing, and it is also wider than the average Dartmoor stream as well as being deeper. Eventually, a place may be found where it is possible to leap the gaps between a couple of large boulders and cross to the other side. The easiest crossing point is at the old sluice at the west end of the neck of the Swincombe Valley. This is definitely preferable to attempting to cross the mire, although in the dry summer of 1982 I recall doing so in wellington boots with no difficulty. More recently, we eventually crossed it on the west side, just avoiding bootfuls of muddy water, but having a marvellous time inducing quakes in the boggy ground for many yards around. Taken on balance (or perhaps off-balance!), I prefer a few short hops across the Swincombe to a prolonged flounder through the mire.

On reaching the opposite bank of the river, we head westwards alongside the wall, crossing from one side to the other by way of a gate. After careful steps through the boggy ground that flanks the Strane River, another gate in the wall leads us south-westwards along the track. We

Ruined mine buildings at Whiteworks.

then pass through the extensive ruins and workings of the Whiteworks Tin Mine. Here, there once stood a large wheel which drove the mining machinery and took its power from water conveyed from a hillside leat along an aqueduct propped on timber supports. The extent of the ruins, which include fenced-off, filled-in shafts, awakens the realisation that this was once a scene of frenetic, noisy activity in great contrast to the brooding silence that now prevails.

To conclude this walk, we now join the narrow metalled road and proceed uphill past the Whiteworks Mine Cottages and the adjoining wind-generator: the cottages, themselves, look only slightly more cheerful than they did in the early 1980s, when their walls were finished grimly in unalleviated black. Thereafter, we soon arrive back at the quarry next to the Devonport Leat, where we began our walk around this sombre stretch of moorland mire.

It is easy to understand how Conan Doyle might have been moved to use the mire as the setting for *The Hound of the Baskervilles*. He may have exaggerated its perils for literary effect, but his inspiration must have come as much from its setting deep below a rectangle of green hills remote from the bustle of daily life, as from the difficult nature of the ground itself. I am, therefore, convinced that this lonely place was, indeed, the reality behind his Great Grimpen Mire. Where else could be *the huge mottled expanse of green-splotched bog which stretched away until it merged with the russet slopes of the moor*? What is more, there is another place nearby, one which we have visited on our walk that conveys the same sense of latent menace as the mire itself. For me, it cements into place the link with the story. Consider Dr Watson's description of his visit to Merripit House with Stapleton and his wife, having met them on the edge of the mire:-

A short walk brought us to it, a bleak moorland house, once the farm of some grazier in the old prosperous days ... the trees, as is usual upon the moor, were stunted and nipped, and the effect of the whole place was mean and melancholy.

The place in question is, indeed, mean and melancholy-looking. It was built in 1901, next to a cottage erected on the site 30 years previously when a farm was first established there by a man named John Hooper. The completion of the newer house came at about the time when *The Hound of the Baskervilles* was first published as a serial in the *Strand* magazine.

Whenever I walk to it, either along the leat or directly over the hill from the road to Princetown, the sudden sight of Nun's Cross Farm instantly brings Conan Doyle's description of Merripit House into my mind.

✳✳✳✳✳

2

FUR TOR

Fur Tor is an imposing stack of granite crowning a rock-strewn hillside. It lies in the wild and desolate heart of northern Dartmoor and, despite, or perhaps because of, its remoteness is regarded as a 'goal' for many walkers on the high moor. Unlike the previous walk to Fox Tor Mire, it is impossible to drive anywhere near it as the closest point accessible by car is Baggator Gate, which lies 2^{1}/$_{2}$ miles away in a straight line. However, do not be deceived – those 2^{1}/$_{2}$ miles may be the shortest distance on the map, but they involve crossing terrain which, when not boggy, is steep; and a well-worn cliché tells us that, on Dartmoor, the most direct route is seldom the quickest.

A walk to Fur Tor is not something which should be contemplated lightly. Besides being enclosed by the Okehampton and Merrivale Firing Ranges, its remoteness, altitude and the rough ground which has to be crossed require the walker to check carefully the weather forecast and, indeed, his or her fitness and equipment before setting off. The position of Fur Tor in the centre of the northern moor means that, theoretically, there are a number of routes which could be followed. In practice, some of these rule themselves out, perhaps because of the very wet and boggy ground which lies in wait, or else due simply to the bone-grinding, ankle-numbing roughness of many of the grassy slopes and hilltops.

I well remember the first time that my wife and I walked out to Fur Tor, blissfully unaware of what was in store. We parked our car in the abandoned quarry opposite the Two Bridges Hotel and set off up the valley of the West Dart, skirting the weird, stunted oaks of Wistman's Wood, crossing the Lich Path and making our way up the southern slopes of Crow Tor. After a pause at the top to lighten the load of the rucksack by drinking some of its contents, the serious work began. Leaving Crow Tor behind us, we made off northwards towards Rough Tor, up one of those endless slopes where the top seems to be for ever on the skyline. Eventually, though, we passed Rough Tor and then dropped down into the valley of the Summer Brook, at Horse Hole. Next we made our way up the eastern slopes of Summer Hill, on to what looked from the map to be an easy, gently-graded plateau towards Fur Tor.

The gateway to the northern moor at Two Bridges.

Our map of this stretch of ground between the heads of the Rivers Cowsic, Tavy and West Dart showed very little apart from one or two contours. It did not prepare us for what we found – 2 miles of unmitigated sweat and slog across a tussocky sea of wind-blown grass, broken only by sudden and irregular holes and trenches where the peat had been dug out long ago. Every step was preceded by the suspense of wondering what tendon-wrenching angle the foot would be forced into as it came down on the next cannonball-sized tussock, or by a mental bracing for the next bone-jarring step into a half-hidden peat cut. In all senses we were treading into the unknown as, heads down, we forced more energy out of muscles groaning for an end to this torture. Then, looking up momentarily from the ground, where all our concentration had been focussed for some while, we suddenly caught sight of a pile of rocks peering over the skyline. As we went on up the gradual slope, more and more of this rock-stack came into view. Finally, we could see Fur Tor in all its glory, and I still have a vivid impression of how it appeared that day – a grey galleon tossed high on a rolling green ocean against the backcloth of a pale, hazy sky.

Lurching painfully across the final few hundred yards of peat hags, we collapsed thankfully on to the rocks at the foot of the main stack, weary with our exertions, but buoyed up by our achievement. When the mist of sweat and fatigue had cleared we sat for a long while, taking in the solitude of Cut Combe Water and Great Kneeset, which appeared every so often through the hazy cloud. We knew that there must be an easier way of getting to Fur Tor than we had chosen that day, but the rigour of our long trek had served to emphasise for us what a remote spot this was.

A rest and a drink are in order before tackling the climb to Fur Tor.

We journeyed back over Devil's Tor, Lydford Tor and Beardown Tor, then descended into the valley of the West Dart and followed the Devonport Leat. Gradually we were leaving behind us the sense of isolation that we had experienced earlier, and by the time that we had reached Beardown Farm and Two Bridges felt just as though we had returned from a journey to the moon.

Despite its bulk, Fur Tor is not visible from any part of the edge of the moor except, briefly, from Black Down, north of Mary Tavy; you have to climb at least one hill, or tor, to be able to see it. Great Mis Tor approaches Fur Tor for magnificence, but is, of course, easily seen from the 'in-country' around the edge of the moor and, indeed, from some way off. In a way, this enhances the sense that Fur Tor is buried deep in the fastness of the moor, forbidden territory to the car-bound tourist.

Two years after our first expedition to Fur Tor, we returned. Remembering all too well our exertions on that previous walk, we decided to try what appeared on the map to be the shortest route. I was further influenced in my choice by the weight of our one-year old son, who was travelling on my back in a carrier. We parked at Baggator Gate and made our way out to Fur Tor by way of Lynch Tor and Fur Tor Brook. Although the going was hard in places, we reached our destination without any traumas of the sort we had gone through before. This time we had a magnificent view northwards to the great tors of north Dartmoor – Yes Tor, High Willhays and Great Links Tor. In addition, down in the valley of the West Okement, we could see the distinctive little rock turret perched on top of Lints Tor. And, throughout most of this, our son slept peacefully in his carrier, awaking only twice; once to have his lunch and once to shed noisy tears as two low-flying military jets flashed over our heads with a penetrating roar! Incidentally, years later, when aged ten, he was able, with his twin eight-year old brothers, to walk out with us from the observation post on Okement Hill to Fur Tor by way of Cranmere Pool. We were proud of the way they managed this arduous journey with only a few complaints. However, it was not the first time they had been on such a tough walk, for 2 years earlier they had all walked to the summits of Snowdon and the Glyders on successive days.

Some ponies seen resting on the north-western slopes of Fur Tor as if contemplating the vastness of their surroundings. On the distant skyline is Great Links Tor.

When viewed from the northernmost heights of the moor, Fur Tor appears on the horizon like the distant throne of some Dartmoor god-king. To its left is the great rounded dome of Cut Hill; although this is higher than Fur Tor by some hundred feet and gives a better view into the far distance, it does not, perhaps because of its more gradual slopes and lack of a rock-stack, have the same brooding, all-dominant presence.

On my most recent visit to Fur Tor I tried out a new route, which took in Cut Hill (it can also be approached from the East Dart Valley and from Tavy Cleave, but I will reserve my impressions of these for later chapters). Leaving home early one summer Saturday, I drove down to Okehampton and up the rough, winding military road which loops out on to the northern moor. Parking at the observation post on Okement Hill at about 8.30a.m., I set off along the track to Hangingstone Hill until, after a short distance, I struck off southwards along the upper Taw Valley and over the watershed to East Dart Head. As I walked, I was conscious that this small area of about 1 square kilometre is the source of several main rivers. Each grows quickly from a small, but persistent, trickle through the thick grass into a tumbling, white-flecked torrent of dark water flowing relentlessly onwards to the distant coasts of North or South Devon. The fate of a single raindrop falling here could be to finish up in the sea at either Dartmouth or Barnstaple (some 55 miles apart), depending on where, within a few yards, it fell on that gentle green crest of the watershed between the East Dart and the Taw.

Skirting the marshy ground near East Dart Head, I climbed the side of Black Hill and headed up the long slope towards Cut Hill, skeins of lank, wet grass trying to check every stride. Soon the sun began to burn off the early morning cloud and, with not a single soul to be seen in any direction, I waded on through the deep tussocky grass, aided by a narrow track left behind by some intrepid group hell-bent on completing the Ten Tors Expedition. Coming across one of the many letterboxes which are secreted on the moor, I was moved by the sheer exhilaration of being there to write in the visitors' book *I am here, the wife and kids are at the mother-in-law's, the sun is shining and God is in His heaven!* Here and now in these pages, I withdraw the part about my close family! But to be able to escape from the routine of daily life to freedom in the depths of Dartmoor on such a day was a truly sublime experience.

Passing over the crest of Cut Hill, I suddenly found myself looking down on to the familiar rocks of Fur Tor, bathed in the hot sunshine of that July morning. One or two distant groups of walkers could be seen making their way towards it, and I hurried on to join them at this remote outpost. The clarity of that fine summer's day showed Fur Tor in all its glory. But it did not give the true essence of this isolated spot. On an overcast day the prospect of this lonely tor jutting out of the upper Tavy fen, backed by an iron-grey sky, drives the fearsome desolation of the northern moor into the walker's psyche. It concentrates the mind; it gives rise to involuntary calculations of whether enough daylight remains for the return journey; it summons up doubt to replace confidence; it is one of the most awe-inspiring sights on Dartmoor.

The main rock-stack of Fur Tor.

✳✳✳✳✳

3

TAVY CLEAVE

When Dartmoor was formed many millions of years ago it resembled a huge granite dome. The gradual, but continuous, action of rain, wind and temperature change on this dome has produced the landscape we see today; the high central parts of the moor remain generally flatter than the outside, having originally been on the top part of the dome. Most of the original upper layers of rock have been worn away. Their remains are to be seen in the form of tors, where the action of the elements has produced some weird and wonderful rock structures that help to give the moor its special character. These tors are, themselves, in a state of imperceptible, but continuous, decay.

The other prominent features have been brought about by the cutting action of water. Rain has fallen on the high parts of the granite dome and, on its way down, has hewn from even the hardest rock a number of deep river valleys. Indeed, anyone walking on Dartmoor will very soon appreciate that water and its effects are a dominant feature of the terrain. Mires and bogs can be found in unexpected as well as obvious places. We have already visited Fox Tor Mire and will, in the course of these pages, venture out to Aune Head Mire. These impressive bowls collect water from the surrounding hills, which is then held back in the grasp of the spongy, peaty soil on the basin floor. There are, however, some places which firmly disprove any notion that water collects only in the valleys. A walk out to Stenga Tor, high on the side of the West Okement Valley, will serve to demonstrate this. The rock-stack is surrounded for many yards by ground which is extraordinarily boggy and difficult to cross, despite its slope. In fact, on many hillsides of Dartmoor one will encounter unexpected areas of bog. These result from rainwater being channelled by both unseen underground rock formations and the visible natural slopes as it flows downhill to the main river below.

The hills and tors of the moor have a character all of their own. To cross them is to experience all the sensations of being in an exposed, remote wilderness in which the wind, the sky and the distant horizon dominate. To descend from these heights into the river valleys is to enter a different world, whose limits are much closer to hand and where water rules. These valleys begin often in gentle, boggy depressions in the high moorland watershed. As water collects at the head of the river, and begins to flow away, the valley grows into a shallow trough. There is little contrast with the surrounding open moorland other than a more sheltered environment and a slight, but sometimes welcome, variation in the landscape. Soon, though, the valley takes on a very distinct nature from the ground above. As the flow of water increases and the burgeoning river cuts down into the underlying rock, it becomes deeper and wider. To the walker, the slopes become a barrier between two quite different worlds. One is restricted to walking alongside the river, or up on the high plateau above, but not in between. The size of the valley makes any walk from the one to the other very arduous, at least until the higher headwaters of the valley are attained.

In many moorland valleys, particularly in those of the Erme, Dart and West Okement, the scale of the slopes between the hills above and the river below quickly becomes vast. In the valley of the Erme, for instance, the distance between Hillson's House and Three Barrows, two high points on opposite sides of the valley, is about a mile and each towers some 750 feet above the tumbling waters at its foot. There is, however, one very notable exception to this tendency towards the rapid formation of wide, deep valleys as I shall explain.

The River Tavy begins high on the slopes of Cut Hill – in the deepest tussock territory through which my wife and I once mistakenly chose to flounder on our first visit to Fur Tor! From its head, it swings first westwards and then, as it drops over a steeper shoulder of Fur Tor, accelerates north-westwards. Collecting its dues in the form of water from Fur Tor Brook and Eastern Red Lake, it hurries on towards the foot of Amicombe Hill, by now flowing almost due north. Merging with the Amicombe Brook at Sandy Ford, it then turns to the west, through one of those little valleys so characteristic of the young rivers of Dartmoor. However, as the waters of Western Red Lake join it from the south, the valley suddenly takes on an altogether different nature; the slopes on either side steepen and appear to be hemming in the river. Then, at yet another confluence, this time with the Rattlebrook, the river rounds a right-angled bend to flow south-westwards and suddenly there is revealed a valley of quite stunning beauty and visual impact.

Tavy Cleave, as this location is named, is very different from other Dartmoor valleys. The distance between the tops of the steep slopes is no more than about half a mile and the depth to the rocky floor averages around 350 feet. In terms of scale, therefore, it is about a quarter of the size of the Erme Valley at Stall Down. But bald statistics alone cannot hope to convey the sublime, light-headed sense of wonderment and surprise instilled by a walk through this gorge alongside the tumbling cadences of the river.

The valleys of the Erme, Dart, West Okement and other Dartmoor rivers all contribute to the variety of a unique landscape. Nevertheless, Tavy Cleave stands alone, unchallenged in its supremacy as a rocky, watery wonderland. Paradoxically, its small size compared to its grander brethren is the vital element of its exceptional beauty. But this still will not suffice. A drab statement of mere dimensions, or a crude comparison with other river valleys must be discarded as futile efforts to convey the characteristics of Tavy Cleave. A walk through it is the only possible way to do it justice, and that is what we must now set out to do.

Leaving the Tavistock to Okehampton road at Mary Tavy and heading along the narrow road that winds up past the Elephant's Nest Inn through Horndon and Willsworthy, one finally reaches the moor gate at Lane Head. Just inside is a small parking area overseen by a standard Army issue flagpole, from which a red flag will fly when the Willsworthy Firing Range is in use. On such days, Tavy Cleave will be out of bounds.

Ger Tor dominates the approach to Tavy Cleave.

Ahead, the skyline is dominated by the heights of Ger Tor, but the path heads almost due eastwards alongside the wall of Nattor Farm. Beyond the farm, we turn slightly north of east and very soon come to the Wheal Friendship Leat; this draws its water from a weir higher up the Tavy and was constructed to drive the machinery in the now long–abandoned Wheal Friendship Copper Mine at Mary Tavy. Nowadays, water from the leat provides the natural power to operate a turbine at Mary Tavy, which generates 3 megawatts of electricity for public use. This turbine, although modest in capacity, is the largest hydro-electric power station in England. The water from the leat is stored in the Wheal Jewel Reservoir so as to enable a constant supply of water to be available when the turbine is in use. At Chagford, on the east side of the moor, there is a much smaller hydro-electric station, generating 30kw of electricity.

I well recall walking with my family through Tavy Cleave one windy, but brilliantly sunny autumn day. We arrived at Lane Head at about 9.00 a.m., followed the leat upstream and, after rounding the slopes of Nat Tor, entered the valley of the Tavy. We took the path along the bank of Wheal Friendship Leat; ahead of us a shoulder of Standon Hill projected into the valley, closing off the view into the Cleave itself. To our right, the Tavy Valley was still quite wide, but as we walked on along the level path the valley quickly became narrower and its floor rose up to meet us. Passing among the rocks by the weir from where the leat draws its water, we found ourselves walking into the narrow valley of Tavy Cleave proper.

The River Tavy sweeps around the right-angled bend in Tavy Cleave.

The scene before us that morning was one which I shall always remember. The sun shone down from a sky so clear that even the dark moorland waters of the Tavy were transformed into a stream of brilliant blue. Flecked now and then with pockets of white water, it tumbled over half-submerged rocks before being soothed into a calmer mood by the deeper, stilling pools. Like a ribbon of pure colour, it painted its way around a random succession of large boulders, which rose up from the stream-bed in a vain effort to halt its onward progress. On either side the slopes were washed in the October brown of decaying bracken, whose uniform shade was spotted grey and white by the clitter scattered over the hillsides. Higher still, the rocky stacks of the Tavy Cleave Tors towered

Tavy Cleave Tors fill the skyline beyond the waterfall.

33

skywards into the blue beyond. In that landscape, against the almost unreal backdrop of such a glorious day, it was easy to imagine oneself being far removed, even from Dartmoor. Surely we would soon round a corner and view some distant mountain from whose dizzy heights the river started its course? Or were we, even as we walked, being observed in our every movement by some hidden horde of bandits, lurking hawk-eyed among the rocks on the skyline and waiting for the right moment to descend upon us?

At one place the river became very shallow as it flowed down a short rocky slope in the valley floor. This gave an unusual and memorable effect. As we continued upstream, we found the water surface of the river ahead flowing towards us at exact eye level, the phenomenon being enhanced by the white-splashed blue reflected from the clear canopy overhead. As we walked on in wonderment, we were slow to notice that the valley was all the while becoming shallower. Soon we were rounding the final bend in the Cleave and ahead we could see the point where the Rattlebrook flowed in from the north. After a rest there,

The rough and tumble of the River Tavy as it pours down into Tavy Cleave below Rattlebrook Foot. Military observation huts scar the profile of Amicombe Hill.

we climbed out of the confined valley world on to the slopes leading to Watern Oke. From there, far away to the north, we could see the normally skulking, gloomy profile of Bleak House lit up almost white in the bright sunshine, but, as always, watched over by its cloying attendants, the Dunnagoats and Green Tor. Climbing higher, the huge promontory of Fur Tor could be seen thrusting its way out of the tussocky levels around Tavy Head.

We were, by now, up on the southern face of Amicombe Hill, part of

The upper entrance to Tavy Cleave, with the Tavy Cleave Tors dominating the skyline.

the longest and most featureless ridge on the whole moor. A glance at the map shows the size and extent of this enormous lump of granite. Its northern slopes soar up out of the West Okement Valley above Meldon Reservoir. Then, rising more gently and taking in Corn Ridge, Lyd Head and Woodcock Hill, it attains its maximum height of 1,916 feet above sea-level near Kitty Tor. For about a mile and a half it then falls southwards at a steady gradient, levels out opposite Little Kneeset and finally drops down to meet the Amicombe Brook and the River Tavy. From here to the foot of its northern slopes is a distance of about 4¹/₂ miles. Although it lacks what would be an apt crown of weather-blown rock, this ridge is a truly gargantuan feature of the moor.

On the slopes of the hill above the Tavy are to be found, half-buried in the long grass, nearly one hundred stone circles comprising the Watern Oke settlement. This Bronze Age settlement was excavated in 1905 by a small army of men under the command of the vicar of Mary Tavy, the Reverend I.K. Anderson. He concluded from his investigations that this site dates from around 1400 BC.

Finally, we had to wrench ourselves away from our perch above this remote and beautiful valley. We could have made our way back alongside the Tavy, but we chose to use up our surplus energy by attacking the slopes of the high ground to the west and heading towards Hare Tor. Once we had attained enough height, a right-angled turn to the south pointed us towards the rock-pile of Ger Tor. We were then back on the more familiar high moorland and, on reaching Ger Tor, our car park could be seen at the foot of the long slope ahead. From this height, Tavy Cleave lay hidden below us, a little paradise on earth which had shared with us its secret wonders and delights. It had been an unforgettable experience.

✳✳✳✳✳

4

RED LAKE

Red Lake spoil tip – it has become a pertinent part of the landscape, a mysterious focal point on this bleak, empty plateau.

Fur Tor, set far out on the northern moor, is a place which draws me irresistibly whenever I venture on to that part of Dartmoor. It is a natural marker of all that is most inaccessible and remote and, by the same token, most worthy of a visit.

On south Dartmoor there is another beacon of the wilderness which blazes forth its presence so prominently that no-one anywhere near can fail to be aware of it. As the eye sweeps around, taking in the emptiness of the central part of the southern moor, it is forever drawn back to settle on the unexpected shape of the Red Lake spoil tip, which rises like some Devonian Ayers Rock out of the vast green desert all around it.

Red Lake China Clay Works is another of those failed Dartmoor ventures whose future had, at the time of inception, seemed so promising for its promoters. It was opened in 1910 and was linked to the clay drying works at Cantrell, near Bittaford, by the Red Lake Tramway. This ran like some sinuous safety rope connecting the Works with the outside world at the southern edge of the moor. China clay, which is decomposed felspar, had, and still has, a key role in the production of paper. The vast china clay works at Lee Moor is a testament to the great importance which this industry has today, but it is a shame that it has to be on Dartmoor, albeit on the edge.

The china clay was extracted by digging out a deep pit at the bottom of which was a tunnel leading to a pump sump at the base of a shaft. High pressure hoses were played on to the sides of the pit in order to wash the clay to the bottom, from where it flowed as a slurry into the pumps. A trap at the base of the pit collected the coarse sand and stones contained in the clay. The trap was emptied periodically by shovelling its contents into trucks lowered into the pit along an inclined railway leading directly down from the side of the spoil tip. This incline is still apparent today, on the western face of the spoil tip.

The clay was pumped away through settling beds to remove mica and finer sand, and then flowed by gravity as a slurry for 7 miles down a twin clayware pipeline to Cantrell. Here, it was dried and loaded on to railway trucks for despatch by means of a siding linked to the nearby main line of the Great Western Railway. The Red Lake Tramway, itself, was 3ft gauge and was used solely for the transport of men and materials to and from Cantrell.

The Works took its name from a stream called Red Lake, which flows from a nearby mire to join the River Erme at the foot of Stingers Hill,

The foundations of the pump engine house at the site of Red Lake China Clay Works.

about a mile away. The term 'lake' can be rather misleading because, on Dartmoor, it is used to refer to a small stream, rather than a broad expanse of water. The ruins of numerous buildings remain at the site of the Works, along with three deep water-filled pits and a bank of grass-covered clay waste. But these are put in their places by the stark, black, volcanic shape of the Red Lake spoil tip which rises like a phoenix from the ashes of the old Works.

Anyone approaching the centre of southern Dartmoor in clear weather from the east, west or north will become aware of the spoil tip from some way off. Its black appearance in dull weather is caused by the thick growth of heather which covers much of its surface. The growth is broken by streaks of white. This is where the heather has been worn down to the coarse sand below by the feet of those who have completed their pilgrimage by walking up to the summit of the spoil tip. Back in the days when the Works was in use, this spoil tip must have been a truly scandalous blemish on the face of the moor. Yet now, paradoxically, with the growth of heather over its white surface, it has become a pertinent part of the landscape, a mysterious focal point on this bleak, empty plateau.

One way of reaching Red Lake is to go out on to the open moor at Harford Moor Gate, above the church. Keeping the little reservoir and the Butter Brook on the right, we climb past the head of the brook and soon reach the long row of boundary stones which runs north-south from Red Lake, itself, down to Western Beacon, near Bittaford. Turning north to follow the boundary stones, the track-bed of the tramway is reached about a third of a mile after the ancient Hobajons Cross. There

Hobajons Cross, on the way up to Red Lake from Harford Moor Gate.

Derek Giles

The track-bed of the former tramway now provides a firm path into the heart of the southern moor.

then follows a long, but easy, walk northwards along the old tramway which, with its steady gradient and even ground, contrasts with the rough grassland on either side.

The Red Lake sand pits, just to the south of Crossways. China clay slurry was pumped from the shaft and discharged through these pits to settle out the light sand. Beyond the sand pits were the Greenhill Micas where mica was removed. Clay slurry then flowed by gravity pipe-line to Cantrell. In the far distance, top right, can be seen the present-day Lee Moor China Clay Works.

As the track-bed winds around the contours past Leftlake Pit (another remnant from the days of china clay extraction), so down below, to the west, the River Erme cuts along the floor of the deep valley which, over countless millennia, it has carved out of the bedrock. Further on, past Quickbeam Hill, more remains of the china clay industry are to be seen in the form of sequential terraces of settling beds. They were used to separate mica and finer sand from the china clay slurry extracted at Red Lake, and are so arranged to make the best use of the natural profile of the ground. The tramway then swings eastwards in its final approach to the clay works whereupon the Red Lake spoil tip suddenly appears to the north as our outward journey nears its end.

From the top of the spoil tip the view to the north is of a huge, gradual slope, taking in Crane Hill, Caters Beam, Green Hill, Nakers Hill and Ter Hill. It is interrupted only by the low ground of Fishlake Mire and the Avon Valley. Ignoring, for a moment of fantasy, the nearby remains of the Works, it is easy to imagine oneself as the first human being ever to set foot on this unbroken green fastness. To the west, the ground dips down towards a little valley through which flow the waters of the upper reaches of the River Erme: to the south, the ridge of Brown Heath shuts off what would otherwise be an extensive view down the Erme Valley: eastwards lies the top of the whale-back of Huntingdon Warren, by way of which there is an alternative route to approach Red Lake from the edge of the moor.

There are two convenient springing-off points for Red Lake on the south-eastern side of the moor. One is at Cross Furzes, where one can park at the roadside and follow the Abbots' Way up on to the moor, skirting the northern flank of the Avon Reservoir and heading up the valley of the River Avon to Huntingdon Cross. The other (better, in my opinion) is just before Hayford Hall, where there is a reasonably wide area to facilitate parking and which can be reached by driving a little further northwards from Cross Furzes and turning into the narrow road leading out to Lud Gate. As one continues on foot, the metalled road soon gives way to a stony track between two walls and bounded on either side by trees: in autumn, the carpet of damp, brown leaves deadens every step and fills the nostrils with the dank, earthy tang of decaying vegetation. At the end of this track the Lud Gate heralds the open moor, the stone walls are quickly left behind and a well defined path leads up the slope and over the ridge between Hickaton Hill and Pupers Hill.

Here we must pause, because I am afraid that I simply cannot resist reverting to the subject of Sir Arthur Conan Doyle's gripping tale, *The Hound of the Baskervilles*. In chapter 1, I wrote of how Fox Tor Mire is thought to have inspired the idea of the Great Grimpen Mire in the story and how Nun's Cross Farm always evokes for me the description of Merripit House, the home of the villain of the piece. But there is an alternative candidate. Looking at the map of the area in which we are walking, I do wonder whether Baskerville Hall was modelled on Hayford Hall, near where we started our walk. It is close to the moor and from it a path leads out to Huntingdon Warren, where a house stood for some 150 years until the 1950s. Could this have represented Merripit House? Its distance from Hayford Hall is certainly one which, a century ago, would have been reasonable for walking home after dining out, as Sir Henry Baskerville did on that climactic night when the hound was finally loosed upon him.

Near Hayford Hall is the village of Combe – Coombe Tracey in the book? But Baskerville Hall is supposed to have been 14 miles from Princetown and, in a straight line, surely Hayford Hall is only 7¹/₂ miles away? Ah yes, but, if you go by road from Hayford Hall to Princetown by way of Holne and Dartmeet the distance is ... 14 miles. And what about where it says in the book that ...? That's enough. I will go no further. I am demolishing my own cherished theories about one of my favourite books. Let's get back to the walk!

The track carries on down to the bottom of the valley, where the Western Wellabrook flows along the foot of Huntingdon Warren. Here, the brook forms the boundary of the Forest of Dartmoor and a small bridge affords an easy crossing into the warren itself. Facing us on the broad-backed hillside are the remains of Huntingdon Warren Farm and its walled enclosures, which were recently renovated. There are also

The enclosure walls at Huntingdon Warren Farm, which were recently renovated. The former site of the house is by the tall sycamore tree.

Above: Huntingdon Cross.

Below: Huntingdon Clapper Bridge.

numerous pillow mounds (or artificial rabbit burrows) bearing testament to the commercial farming of rabbits that was practised on Dartmoor for many hundreds of years and survived until well into the 20th century: some of the other, better-known, warrens were at Ditsworthy, Trowlesworthy and Hen Tor in the Plym Valley and also at Headland and Soussons near Postbridge. The warren at Huntingdon, which was established in the early 19th century and extended over some 500 acres, ceased to operate at some time in the 1920s, but the warren house continued to be occupied for another 30 years or so. In 1956, however, it was gutted by fire and in 1961 it was demolished, its only link with the outside world having been the track that we have been following.

The direct route from here to Red Lake, in fact, lies westwards over the top of Huntingdon Warren, but I would advise against this because it includes some of the worst, foot-wrenching, grassy tussockland on the whole moor. My family and I discovered this when returning from Red Lake to Lud Gate one July in a prolonged spell of squall-driven, horizontal rain. Every stride was an effort; the long grass tugged at our feet, frequently tripping us, as we tried to keep some semblance of direction through the low cloud with the aid of the compass and all the while the rain drenched into our backs. Then, having struggled on over the hill to Lud Gate, eventually reaching the shelter of our car, the rain stopped abruptly and the sun emerged hot from behind the clouds. Five steaming, exhausted figures stripped off furtively behind the car and changed into dry clothes!

As a result of this experience I am bound to say that it is better to stay on the eastern side of the Western Wellabrook and follow it southwards past the ruins of Keble Martin's Chapel. This is named after the Reverend F. Keble Martin, the author of that classic work *The Concise British Flora in Colour*. He grew up knowing Dartmoor well and, as a young clergyman, baptised the child of the warrener while camping here with his brothers.

A path continues close to the bank of the stream with the looming, hunched slopes of Huntingdon Warren to the right. The ancient form of Huntingdon Cross can now be seen, close to where the waters of the Western Wellabrook meet those of the River Avon. This spot, sheltered in the narrow valley, always fills me with a potent awareness that man has been passing this way for many hundreds of years. This feeling is instilled first by the knowledge that, in 1240, the perambulation of the Forest of Dartmoor was carried out by twelve knights, whose journey took them past this very spot. Then there is the brooding presence of the cross, which was erected on the Forest boundary in the mid-16th century; also the Abbots' Way (that path of indeterminate age and more accurately known here as the Jobbers' Road), which runs hard by the cross on its way over the moor, reputedly between the abbeys of Buckfast and Tavistock. On the nearby slopes of Huntingdon Warren and Hickaton Hill there remain to this day numerous hut circles and enclosures. These have lain undisturbed ever since ancient man chose to settle here. Another, more recent, reminder of the works of man is the little clapper bridge that spans the Avon a short distance upstream, this having been erected by the warrener so that he might more easily attend to those of his charges whose burrows were on the other side of the river.

We must now brace ourselves to leave this valley by way of the steep slope of the ridge separating the valleys of the Avon and the Erme, and which is crowned by the ancient Eastern and Western Whittabarrows: the former is visible from miles around and its distinctive shape makes it look for all the world like one of those early submarines. Although this is a stiff climb, it is also a comparatively short one, and by following the Abbots' Way directly up the side of the ridge we soon arrive at Crossways, where the path crosses the track-bed of an old tramway. Built in the last century, this served to carry peat, dug from nearby workings, on a 3-mile journey down to Shipley Bridge. Here, there was a processing works for extracting naptha from the peat – a venture which did not take long to prove unviable.

Looking to the north, we can now, at last, see the Red Lake spoil tip rearing up unexpectedly like some blackened, malignant growth upon the otherwise unblemished body of this virgin landscape. It gives an insight to the attitudes that prevailed even into the earlier part of this century. In his single-minded urge to extract some commercial benefit from the moor, the original promoter of this china clay works was clearly highly motivated. He was even prepared to lay a 7-mile long tramway to the middle of the southern moor, like a lance into its heart, and to erect his works at one of the highest and most exposed places imaginable. Production of china clay then took place from 1913 until 1932, apart from certain interruptions during the years 1915 and 1922 caused by problems brought on by the Great War, such as reduced demand and shortage of labour. The depression of the early 1930s, however, brought about the eventual demise of the venture, a situation that from the point of view of protecting the moor from further damage was most fortunate because the extensive china clay deposits at Red Lake were far from worked out.

Nowadays, it seems remarkable that the final owners of the Works made no effort, in a period of cheap labour, to remove the spoil, or even to level it out, when the Works were finally abandoned. That the owners of the land, the Duchy of Cornwall, neither insisted that it be removed nor did so themselves by default, is even more difficult to understand. It could so easily have been pushed back into one of the very deep pits, now filled with water, from where it came. That said, time and nature have joined forces to soften its impact with a covering of heather. This, in turn, has created for Dartmoor a tangible reminder to any would-be invaders of its sanctity that others have tried, but have failed.

✳✳✳✳✳

5

ERME PITS

The area known as the Forest of Dartmoor encompasses 77 square miles of the highest and most remote parts of the moor. The origins of its boundary come to us, not in some half-forgotten piece of handed-down folklore, but in hard, 700-year old documentary evidence. I remember being taught at school that the word 'forest' did not mean a wooded area – it was a royal hunting ground. This, indeed, is the origin of the Forest of Dartmoor: the earliest known such reference to Dartmoor is in a Charter of 1204, which restricted afforested land in Devonshire to Dartmoor and Exmoor. The location of the Forest boundaries of Dartmoor at that time is not known, but, on 13th June 1240, Henry III issued a writ ordering that the extent of the Forest of Dartmoor should be determined by a perambulation to define its boundaries. The perambulation was to be undertaken by a jury of twelve knights summoned by the Sheriff of Devon, and it was duly carried out shortly afterwards.

I have often speculated idly to myself about this perambulation and its circumstances. Was the Sheriff of Devon besieged by volunteers eager to spend a few days in the fresh air of the moor? Probably not. I assume that in those days knights were fairly few and far between – perhaps it was indeed necessary to formally summon eligible people before they would agree to participate. I suppose that it would have depended on the time of year and the weather. Had the Sheriff of Devon been possessed by a malicious sense of humour, might he possibly have waited until autumn brought the sort of lashing rain that is beating against the window even as I write before issuing a summons to twelve knights to whom he had taken a particular dislike? In fact, he appears not to have been the type of person who might indulge himself in such subtle vengeance. In his return to the King, the Sheriff states that the perambulation was made on the Eve of St James the Apostle, that is the 24th July, 1240, only a few weeks after the King's writ had been issued. This date may actually have been the date on which the perambulation was completed. The circumference of the defined boundary was around 50 miles and, no doubt, there would have been pauses for discussion and debate about the route of the boundary. It seems certain that the perambulation would have taken several days to complete.

How did the knights know where they were during the perambulation? Did they know the terrain intimately through years of hunting the ground by royal invitation? Or were they guided by some unsung local yeoman? If so, had his familiarity with the moor been gained by illicit poaching of the King's venison, at great risk of some draconian and unmentionable amputation?

Were the knights paid to perambulate, or were they summoned in the expectation that they would perform the duty purely out of a deep-rooted sense of loyalty to the Crown? Where did they stay overnight? Most likely they rode off the moor each day to stable their horses and themselves in the relative comfort of some convenient manor house or castle `– it is very hard to imagine them and their retinue of servants camping out on the moor.

How easily did they manage to agree among themselves on the location of the boundary? Did they dutifully ride over every inch of it, or did they get bored with the whole thing and fix some of the boundary around the dinner table? Probably, they sensibly chose the former option, in fear of any dereliction of duty being betrayed to the King. Did they have to check on army firing times before venturing on to ... that's enough. What started as speculation has now become flippancy! At any rate, the boundary fixed by those twelve knights passed, by way of various streams, rivers and notional straight lines, through the following points, of which the modern name is stated in brackets:–

Hoga de Cossdonne	(Cosdon Beacon)
Parva Hunde Torre	(Hound Tor)
Thurlestone	(The Thirlstone on Watern Tor)
Wotesbrokelakesfote	(confluence of Hew Lake with the Teign)
Heighestone	(Longstone – possibly)
Langestone	(Heath Stone – possibly)
Furnum Regis	(King's Oven)
Along the Walla Brook to the East Dart	
Along the East Dart to confluence with West Dart	
Up the West Dart	
Okebrokesfote	(confluence of O Brook with the Dart)
Up the O Brook to confluence with Dry Lake	
Up the Dry Lake	
Dryework	(tin workings by Dry Lake)
Dryfeldford	(intersection of boundary with Sandy Way)
Battyshull	(Ryder's Hill)
Head of Western Wellabrook	
Down the Western Wellabrook to confluence with the Avon.	
Ester Whyteburghe	(Eastern Whitebarrow)
La Rede Lake	(Red Lake)

Down Red Lake to confluence with the Erme
Grymesgrove   (Erme Head – probably)
Elysburghe   (Eylesbarrow)
Syward's Cross   (Siward's or Nun's Cross)
Ysfother   (South Hessary Tor)
Mystor   (Great Mis Tor)
Mewyburghe   (White Barrow – probably)
Lullingesfote   (Limsboro Cairn on Lynch Tor)
Rakernebrokysfote   (Rattlebrook Foot)
Up the Rattlebrook to its head
La West Solle   (Stenga Tor)
Ernestorre   (Yes Tor)
Ford (on the East Okement) east of the Chapel of St Michael of
Halgestoke   (Halstock)
Hoga de Cossdonne   (Cosdon Beacon)

(In some cases the modern name quoted is one of several possible locations that have been suggested by scholars as the position of some of those wonderfully-named places. My favourite, Wotesbrokelakesfote, presumably became corrupted to Hew Lake Foot by the same process which, nowadays, results in the inhabitants of the Devon village of Woolfardisworthy referring to it as 'Woolsery'!)

In 1608 a further perambulation was carried out. This followed the survey of 1240 very closely, but some additional boundary points were defined. Certain interpretations were placed on the previous names and these have added to the confusion and debate about their exact location. The result is that there is some difference between the historical boundary of the Forest and that now officially recognised by the Duchy of Cornwall, which owns the land.

The modern boundary of the Forest happens to pass through my favourite place on the whole of the moor, Erme Pits. This place also means a lot to me in other ways for it was the destination on the first walk which I undertook in a day's visit from home. It was this visit that proved to me that a trip to the moor from Hampshire for a day's walking was a practical proposition.

Erme Pits lies in a little valley at the head of the River Erme, right out in the middle of the southern moor. Like Fur Tor, there is no short route to it – the privilege of being there has to be earned by some fairly hard walking. I shall describe my preferred route to Erme Pits as I found it on that frosty November Saturday when I made my first day trip to the moor.

I had decided to go to the moor, weather permitting, during the preceding week. Every day I had watched the evening weather bulletin hoping, in vain, for a forecast beyond the following day that might give me some inkling of whether or not the trip was going to be on. The longer range forecast available by telephone had been vague and non-committal, so I could not make the final decision until the Friday evening, when the forecast for the south-west was for an overnight frost, followed by a reasonably dry day. Even then I had been slightly apprehensive at the thought of driving 175 miles early in the morning on potentially icy roads, and only when my wife had commented that I should go and get the whole thing out of my system was my mind finally made up.

The alarm went off at four o' clock on Saturday morning and I was up immediately. It is strange how, when I have to get up at an early hour for some special occasion, I tend to wake up just before the alarm goes off, as if prompted by some internal body clock. After a quick cup of tea I left home at a quarter to five and headed over the downs towards Winchester to join the A303 trunk road to the west. This time of day is grand for quick journeys and no delays. By seven o' clock, I was pulling in to the Little Chef near Honiton for a large, cooked breakfast, something I find essential to set me up for a day's walking. Or, maybe, the walk just provides a good excuse for a bit of self-indulgence!

By now, the sky behind me was beginning to glow with the approach of the rising sun. It is an exhilarating feeling to be out and about at that time of day with the brightening sky of a fine morning all around. It is enhanced by the prospect of a long walk and the knowledge that the shackles of routine have been broken, at least for one day.

I reached Princetown at a quarter past eight and rang home to say that I had arrived safely. During the previous night I had written down for my wife the details of the route that I planned to follow, and the time by which I expected to get back to the car. I was pretty confident that the weather would be fine and was, in any case, sure of my ability to navigate on the moor in cloud or fog. But there is always the risk, when walking alone, of breaking an ankle and being unable to summon help. Simple precautions like these cause no inconvenience; but you must not deviate from the pre-arranged route.

After driving out to Whiteworks and parking in the abandoned quarry, I set off along the bank of the Devonport Leat towards Nun's Cross Farm. Reaching the Abbots' Way where a small bridge carries it over the leat, I headed eastwards to where the track fords Nun's Cross Brook, which flows down from the old tin workings above the farm. Normally, the ground on either side would consist of squelchy mud, but on this frosty day the mud had frozen into a hard crust, making the going unexpectedly firm. I swung round to the south-east, proceeded up the slopes of Hand Hill, the morning sun shining full into my face with a brightness so dazzling that it hurt, and paused to recover my breath by the little cross set in the boulder near the top.

It was a brilliantly clear, sunny day. The grass under my feet was crisp

The tiny cross on Hand Hill.

and white as I continued on down the hill into the Plym Valley. Crossing the river at Plym Ford, I carried on up the long slope of Great Gnat's Head, which loomed in front of me. Another pause at the top, and it was time to take a bearing to get me to Broad Rock, one of the significant boundary stones on this part of the moor. Off I went again, disturbing a pair of red grouse into a low, cackling flight over the hill.

According to the map, Broad Rock lies next to the Abbots' Way (more accurately called the Jobbers' Road), but the position of this track on the ground near here is often more imagined than real. At any rate, Broad Rock is almost exactly due south (magnetic south, that is) of the cairn on Great Gnats Head. It marks the boundary of the parish of Cornwood and the Forest of Dartmoor, and is inscribed 'BB Broad Rock'; the initials BB stand for Blachford Bounds, that is, the boundary of the manor of Blachford, near Cornwood, which also passes through this point.

Broad Rock.

South-eastwards from Broad Rock the slope steepened and, at last, I could see ahead the valley of the Erme. Having crossed some rather boggy ground through which the infant river trickles from the nearby hillside, I came to the weird, grass-shrouded spoil heaps of Erme Pits. It is believed that a tin mine existed here as early as the 16th century and certainly the tin workings here are among the most dramatic on the whole moor.

The earliest record of tin mining on Dartmoor dates from 1197. At that time the value of the Devon Stannary was reckoned to be greater than that of Cornwall. Just as the Crown controlled the hunting of deer in the Forest, so did it have a major hold over the mining of tin on the moor, being entitled to receive the profits. The mining process changed little over the centuries. The tin ore was first crushed, by stamps driven by a water-wheel, into particles the size of sand grains. It was then separated from other crushed material by streaming, a process that involved allowing water, perhaps brought in by a leat taken off a river upstream of the mine, to wash the ground-up rock through settling pits, or buddles. Here the heavier ore would settle out and the waste material would be carried away by the water. The streaming waste was washed into a nearby river and, in due course, found its way down to the sea. This is known to have caused problems at Plymouth, where, in 1542, the harbour was found to be silting up as a result of tin mine waste being brought down from Dartmoor with the waters of the River Plym.

There are also several recorded instances of disputes between the tin mine owners and the water supply authorities, who, naturally, wanted a steady, sufficient supply to flow along their leats. However, the mine owners would often, without warning, divert water from the leats, themselves, or from the streams that fed them in order to provide more power for the water-wheels that worked the mine machinery. A long-running dispute, in which the tables were turned, so to speak, arose between the Whiteworks Mine Company and the Devonport Water Company. The cause was the latter's diversion, in 1869, of water into the Devonport Leat from a stream which flowed into the south side of Fox Tor Mire. This deprived the mine of water to the extent that, according to the owners, only about a quarter of the tin-stamps would work properly. The dispute was never satisfactorily resolved, and the reduction in water supply to the mine may have been indirectly responsible for its eventual closure in the early years of the 20th century.

The tin ore was smelted in a furnace by burning peat, which provided a very effective heat and was often, of course, available close by. The smelting furnaces were set up inside stone buildings, the numerous ruins of which remain in many parts of the moor, even in some very remote spots. The process was aided by large bellows powered by a water-wheel, which forced air through the furnace. The smelting buildings

Erme Pits. Note the presence of the Red Lake spoil tip looming on the distant horizon, beyond the gash in the hillside.

consequently became known as blowing-houses. Molten ore was poured into moulds to form ingots and some of the mould-stones are still to be found in, or near, the remains of the blowing-houses.

At one time the area around Erme Pits must have presented an unsightly mess, but the passing of time has reduced the impact of the mounds by covering them with a grassy blanket. In some areas between the mounds, summer will cover the floor with a carpet of short, grazed grass, which looks for all the world as though it is tended daily by some upland park-keeper. This contrasts vividly with the haphazard scattering of rocks and heaps of stone that are to be found around the outside of the mounds and on either side of the river. Just east of the spoil heaps, a rocky, steep-sided gully branches off into the hillside. This gully is another remnant of the tin mining era; its banks are now infested with rabbits.

In this area the modern boundary of the Forest of Dartmoor comes from the east along Red Lake, up the Erme to a stone known as the 'A' Stone, then to Broad Rock and northwards to Plym Head. The 'A' Stone is to be found at grid reference SX621673, in an area known to the perambulators of 1240 as Grymesgrove. This was one of the points defining their boundary and is generally believed to be the marshy area to the north of Erme Head. The stone is inscribed 'A Head', which is believed to denote 'Arme Head', Arme being the old name for Erme. Although some distance from the area shown on modern maps as Erme Head, there is no real reason why this marshy area should not have equal claim to be at the head of the river. The 'A' Stone can be found by walking some 300 to 350 paces (depending on your stride) on a bearing of 88 degrees from Broad Rock. It is a long, low, lozenge-shaped rock, aligned approximately north-south, with a patch of green lichen on its

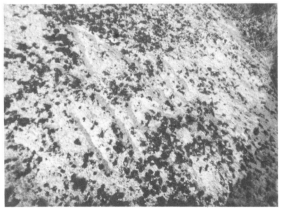

The 'A' Stone. The inscription reads 'A Head', denoting the head of the River Arme (or Erme).

surface, and is located inside a boggy stretch of long wetland grass. The inscription 'A Head' is on the southern end and is more difficult to see in the middle of a sunny day.

For me, the presence of these inscribed stones, Broad Rock and the 'A' Stone, out at this remote spot is a powerful evocation of the long-dead generations of man who have walked, ridden and hunted over the moor. For them it was so important that even here they took the trouble to inscribe these rocks to provide incontrovertible proof of the position of the hunting bounds.

On this particular day I continued on downstream along the left bank of the Erme. Although this valley is in the most remote part of the southern moor, the scene before me, far from being bleak and threatening, was one of almost idyllic tranquillity. Not a soul was to be seen in any direction. The sun shone down from a near-cloudless sky, cattle and horses grazed the short, springy, well-drained turf on the slopes ahead, and the river chattered away into the distance along the marshy floor of the gentle upland valley.

Blacklane Brook.

A few hundred yards downstream I turned northwards into the little narrow valley of the Blacklane Brook. If anything this surpasses the Erme for natural beauty and, shortly after passing the remains of a little blowing-house near a narrow path that wends its way up the west bank of the brook, I chose to pause for lunch by Phillpott's Cave. It had been a frosty night and a persistent chilly breeze had penetrated one or two layers of clothing on the exposed slopes higher up. But down here, in the shelter of the valley, I sat and steamed. My wax jacket and sweater were soon draped over a rock, while I lay back at peace with the world, unable to believe my luck at being out here on such an exhilarating day. Eventually, though, I had to press on, ever mindful of the short daylight hours of November. I knew that I was now past the pinnacle of the walk and must concentrate on getting back. To someone like myself making a brief day's visit to the moor from as far off as Hampshire, this was a slightly depressing moment, but the gloom soon lifted at the thought of a pleasant trek back. I went on up Blacklane Brook and veered round to the west, skirting Ducks Pool, where I saw other people for the first time that day, hunting out the various letterboxes which are hidden in the area. On the south side of the pool is the original Ducks Pool letterbox which was put out in memory of the well-known Dartmoor gazetteer and author, William Crossing, who died in 1928.

The plaque commemorating the life of William Crossing. It is mounted on a large boulder on the south side of Ducks Pool.

Heading almost due west, I continued on towards Great Gnats Head and then back down to Plym Ford, retracing my steps from earlier in the day. For a bit of variety I struck off directly up the slope ahead towards Eylesbarrow Cairn, passing the overgrown remnants of the Wheal Katherine Mine which, long ago, the tin miners had hewn from the hillside. The ground became awkward with boggy areas overlain by long grass, and I began to wish that I had followed the track around the hill towards the old Eylesbarrow Mine. But soon the latest piece of artistry in stone was visible ahead, where some passing walker had erected a personal 'Stonehenge' using some of the mass of small rocks that lie around the Eylesbarrow Cairn. I was now back on the boundary of the Forest of Dartmoor and followed its straight course back towards Nun's Cross, past the numerous Plymouth Corporation Water Works boundary stones erected in 1917 to mark the catchment boundary of Burrator Reservoir, 2 miles to the west.

By now, daylight was starting to fade, prompted by some heavy clouds which obscured the setting sun. I hurried on past Nun's Cross Farm and along the Devonport Leat to the quarry where I had parked many hours before. Down below me the huge, dark bowl of Fox Tor Mire loomed through the gathering dusk and I arrived back at the car conscious that I had cut things rather too fine. I was also conscious of the fact that I now needed to drive quickly back to Princetown in order to telephone home and tell my wife that she would not, after all, have to call out the Mountain Rescue Service! That done, I was able to drive home content in the knowledge that I had cracked the problem of how to get out on to the moor throughout the year. I had also enjoyed an inspiring day's walk. Given good weather, a walk out to any spot within the boundary of the Forest of Dartmoor should be an uplifting experience, and so it had proved. Tomorrow would bring a long lie-in with the Sunday papers, followed by a week back in the routine of work.

Since that day I have had many memorable walks out to Erme Pits. One that sticks in the mind is an autumn journey undertaken in a group of six from the ford on Sheepstor Brook, north of Gutter Tor. The outward route lay over Whittenknowles Rocks to Plym Steps and up the valley of the Langcombe Brook to the kistvaen, or stone burial chamber, known as Grims Grave, which lies within a tight circle of small standing stones; this is another of those prehistoric remains whose preservation to this day never ceases to amaze me. From Grims Grave, the path turned north-eastwards over the lip of Broad Mead, the long ridge between Great Gnats Head and Langcombe Hill, and down into the upper Erme Valley. We then paused in the shelter of Erme Pits for the obligatory refreshment stop – coffee for the adults and fizzy lemonade (shaken to exploding point in our backpacks) for the children – prior to turning for home. On the return journey we searched out the 'A' Stone and Broad Rock before heading back over the shoulder of Great Gnats Head to Plym Ford, and from there took the well-used track running westwards past the old Eylesbarrow Mine.

We watched the autumn sun set behind Bodmin Moor and soon the twilight was creeping up on us. The wind had dropped to nothing and the slender crescent of the new moon dominated the darkening sky above Shavercombe Head. In the gathering gloom, the stillness of the moor around us was palpable. We hurried on to our cars, keenly aware of how the vastness of the moor was emphasised by darkness. It felt as if we, mere mortals, had no right to be there intruding upon the moor's eternally secret night world. But on that day, as on so many others, we had escaped routine to find freedom and peace of mind at Erme Pits in the middle of southern Dartmoor.

❋❋❋❋❋

6

THE EAST DART VALLEY

By now, it should be clear to anyone reading this book that there is a common theme running through all the walks which I have described. Put simply, that theme is my desire to go where nobody else goes or, at least, where nobody else goes very frequently and, if they do, not in crowds. As I explained in my Introduction, I believe that Dartmoor's landscape is one where I can fulfil my frequent need to break free from the grip of routine. However, with the best will in the world, this need cannot be satisfied, even on Dartmoor, at places like Widecombe, Hay Tor, Hound Tor, Dartmeet or Postbridge. Too many people go there.

Whenever I see crowds at these 'honey pots', particularly Dartmeet and also Postbridge, where they gather by the clapper bridge on hot summer days to paddle in the East Dart, I find myself wondering why people go out on to Dartmoor to do this sort of thing. They are missing out on experiencing the real beauty of the moor which is so close at hand. But then, I realise that to have such crowds at Cranmere or Red Lake would be rather incongruous and would take away the magic of these places.

Oddly enough, when setting off in summer up the East Dart, it is the walker arriving in his or her car at Postbridge who feels out of place. Putting on walking boots, packing precautionary waterproofs into a rucksack and tramping self-consciously off across the car park, one can read the thought in the eyes of the owners of all those trainer-shod feet; 'Where on earth is that lunatic off to on a hot day like this?' At times such as these the moorland walker must have a thick skin; he must stride confidently away with an expression conveying sympathy for the poor victims who have succumbed to the meagre attractions of the ice-cream van and the gift shop!

Once away from Postbridge, the East Dart River is followed upstream on its eastern bank by means of a well-defined path that skirts the gentle slope of Hartland Tor and then continues almost exactly due north. On the opposite bank the steeper and more substantial slopes of Broad Down climb away to the west, and it is often above this hill that one can see a buzzard or two soaring high in the sky on the lookout for the next meal. These birds are common on the moor and have a peculiar grace of their own. They have a lazy, but menacing, gliding flight suspended on broad, square-tipped wings which, every so often, condescend to flap a couple of times in the prevailing wind in order to restore the bird's height and direction.

The valley of the East Dart above Roundy Park. Note, to the right of the picture, the western slopes of Hartland Tor blackened by recent swaling.

Eventually, the East Dart Valley does something very peculiar – it sweeps dramatically around to the west through some 135 degrees. This, in turn, means switching quite abruptly, from a northerly to a south-westerly direction, if we are to continue walking upstream, and finding a suitable place to cross Lade Hill Brook, as well as the river itself. Once across to the south bank of the East Dart it is well worth taking stock of the surroundings, particularly the narrowing gorge of the river as it disappears away to the south-west. To the novice walker, the valley of the East Dart is a corridor of certainty. It leads one out to the middle of the northern moor in confidence, through what can otherwise be a rather featureless landscape where, even in clear conditions, deviation from the right direction is all too easy.

Half a mile along the closed world of this valley is a rather beautiful waterfall, a good place to stop for rest and refreshment. Thereafter, it is better to stay on the south side of the river in order to avoid the boggy ground which, otherwise, would be encountered later. Soon the constriction of Sandy Hole Pass appears ahead, the valley becoming ever shallower as we walk further upstream.

A quarter of a mile beyond Sandy Hole Pass the valley suddenly widens out on the northern side, forming a boggy basin known as Broad

Looking downstream through Sandy Hole Pass. The river-bed here is thought to have been deepened by the tinners so as to improve the drainage of their upstream workings.

Marsh. At this point, on the west side of Broad Marsh, the East Dart should be crossed so as to avoid Cut Hill Stream and Cut Lane Stream, which empty into it a short way on. Where the more northerly of these streams, Cut Lane Stream (not Cut Hill Stream as shown on the O.S. map), joins the East Dart, there is a little waterfall known as Kit Steps.

We are now in one of the most remote and tucked away parts of the

Broad Marsh, with Cut Hill behind.

northern moor. Above us to the west are Flat Tor, West Dart Head and the great dome of Cut Hill, which, from our position, however, cannot be fully appreciated. To the east is Winney's Down. Up on these hilltops one can, in the right conditions, see a long way across the moor to other prominent landmarks. But, down here by the East Dart, those same hills form a barrier, enclosing us in our own secluded world with no other soul in view. Like the tourists at Postbridge, we are enjoying the beauty of the East Dart: unlike them, our experience is enhanced immeasurably by being out on our own, remote from civilisation.

From here I like to head towards the prominent outcrop of Kit Rocks on the east bank of the East Dart. This is a good place for a rest and to bask in the feeling of being a free spirit in the wilderness. The river valley continues northwards towards the watershed between the East Dart and the Taw, some 2 miles away, becoming smaller all the time. On either side, as it heads north, are those high, lonely guardians of the fastness of the northern moor – Cut Hill, Black Hill and Whitehorse Hill.

Recently my family and I went out to Kit Rocks on a fine spring day. As we arrived a flock of small moorland birds, mostly pipits and wheatears, came over the hill in hot pursuit of a larger bird. At first we thought that this was a hobby because it had a hawk-like tail, but a closer study of its flight revealed it to be a cuckoo. Presumably it had been caught in the act of trying to lay an egg in a pipit's nest and was, for once, getting the worst of it from this avian neighbourhood watch!

From Kit Rocks, there are one or two options open – perhaps to head on up the valley into the remotest part of the moor at East Dart Head, maybe deviating to Cut Hill and Fur Tor, or perhaps walk out to Whitehorse Hill and Hangingstone Hill. If the weather was fine and there was plenty of daylight left, I would certainly find one of these choices hard to resist. On the other hand, if, because of shortage of time or energy, Kit Rocks is a suitable point at which to turn for home, the quiet and sheltered seclusion of the valley can be forsaken for the gusty heights of the hills. From Kit Rocks, a convenient destination is Statts House at the top of the high ground to the east, on a compass bearing (because you won't see it from Kit Rocks) of 110 degrees. Statts House, by name, is somewhat grander than the reality; it is the small, rectangular, ruined home of a 19th century peat-cutter.

Near Statts House is one of the several peat passes to be found on the northern moor. Like some other peat passes it has a small iron plaque set on a marker stone, telling us that 'This stone marks a crossing through the peat which may be of use to hunters and cattlemen; the crossing was made by Frank Phillpotts who died October 1909. It is kept up in his memory by his brother and son'. These days the peat passes, found only on the northern moor (with the exception of Black Lane above Fox Tor) and of which ten are shown on the O.S. 1:25,000 map, are primarily of

The ruins of Statts House.

use to riders and walkers. The most well-known is North West Passage on Cut Hill, whilst the most useful (and the longest) runs north-south over Black Ridge. After a heavy plod over a long tussocky slope the peat passes, with their even and surprisingly firm going, give a welcome respite and a boost to the walker's morale.

The marker stone at the end of Phillpotts peat pass near Statts House.

Standing by Statts House, the view eastwards is dominated by Sittaford Tor, and we must now make for this landmark. Heading gently downhill, we cross the Maish Hill Brook, which discharges into the young River Teign at Little Varracombe, and then follow our eyes to the top of Sittaford Tor. When we were last there, in April 1994, various groups of teenagers were being checked through on a dry run (admittedly not an appropriate term for a practice walk on Dartmoor) for the annual Ten Tors Expedition, an event first held in 1960. It had been inspired by an army captain by the name of Joyner, who, a year earlier, had been camped out at Teignhead Farm supervising a military exercise, and had conceived the idea of a similar trek for younger people.

I envied those teenagers their long walk over the moor and, judging from their faces, most of them were enjoying themselves, helped, no doubt, by being in groups. However, I did not envy them their huge backpacks full of camping gear, which must become a real handicap to the enjoyment of a walk after a few miles. I was pleased as well that, unlike them, we did not have to spend that night camping on the moor. I have never in my life slept in a tent. I will put up with nearly any discomfort brought on by a good long walk on Dartmoor, but at the end of it I need a long hot soak and a hot meal to round off the day, followed by a sound sleep. Nothing but the most calm, warm and otherwise favourable conditions would induce me even to consider sleeping in a tent on the moor. I do concede, though, that to wake up early on a warm, sunny morning at Huntingdon Warren or Erme Pits must be a truly wonderful experience, at least until you have to pick that backpack up again!

The view from Sittaford Tor is extensive on a clear day, particularly to the south. Most of all, though, I like the prospect of the nearby valley of the North Teign, which has a distinct air of mystery about it. On the opposite slope about half a mile away, backed by a plantation of mostly-felled conifers, is the site of Teignhead Farm. This was built around 1808 and was occupied by a succession of tenants, some of them families with several children, until it was requisitioned by the War Department in November 1942. After the war the farmhouse, damaged by military exercises, was never officially occupied again and its condition deteriorated over the years until, in 1971, it was finally demolished.

A further quarter of a mile northwards down the valley from the site of Teignhead Farm lie the ruins of Manga Farm. This was built at about the same time as Teignhead Farm, but saw far less service as a home than the latter; the last recorded occupancy is in 1871 and, by 1884, it was reportedly in ruins. It is a sobering thought that people chose to try and extract a living out of this exposed and inhospitable terrain, often not to support just one or two people but also a number of children.

The route back to Postbridge from Sittaford Tor is, initially, eastwards. This leads us over the 7-mile long Vitifer Mine Leat – whose waters, taken off the East Dart (as well as off some tributaries of the North

Teign), once drove the water-wheels of the extensive tin mines at Vitifer and Birch Tor – and on towards the Grey Wethers standing out prominently on the valley floor ahead. After inspecting these twin stone circles, with the ranks of the Fernworthy conifers glowering at us over the hilltop beyond, we then turn southwards along the wide green path which runs through them and on down the valley of Lade Hill Brook.

Part of the Grey Wethers double stone circle.

After another mile we pass close by one of the beehive huts which are to be found on the moor; these are generally believed to be associated with the old tin mining industry, perhaps being used for storage of tin ingots. At this stage we are already back in the valley of the East Dart and can return to Postbridge by taking the higher ground over the top of Hartland Tor. If it is summer we may find that on our arrival back at the car park most of the tourists who were there when we set out have headed home – with not a thought for the eccentric-looking person whom they saw striding off across the moor in heavy walking boots so many hours ago! Hopefully they have enjoyed themselves on what they would call a good day out on the moor. But their destination was merely our beginning; we have been able to appreciate the remote, unspoilt beauty of the real Dartmoor, which for those trippers was, and probably always will be, something beyond the hill.

✳✳✳✳✳

7

BLEAK HOUSE

In many places along the edge of Dartmoor the transition from wilderness to civilisation happens gradually as one descends from the heights. But in the north-west, around Sourton, the high moor sweeps across from the east and drops suddenly down; there is an immediate change from bleak moorland to the more usual Devonshire landscape of small fields surrounded by hedgerows and carpeted in lush pasture. Here, the hills nearly always seem to be dark and forbidding, often for no other reason than the sun being behind them for most of the day. Consequently, anyone driving along the road from Okehampton to Tavistock looks up into the gloom of their shadows. Particularly stark are the heights of the Sourton Tors, which loom menacingly over the little village of the same name.

All in all, this is an appropriate place from which to set out on a walk over the moor to a place known as Bleak House, about whose origins I shall say something when we arrive there. As we will see, the walk reveals the traces of a variety of industries that man introduced on to the moor, all to no avail. Just as the scale of these industries varied, so did the length of time it took to realise the hopelessness of their continuance.

The starting point for this walk is the tiny village green at Sourton, almost opposite The Highwayman Inn. From here a stony track leads up the hill past the church and over a bridge which spans the forlorn and overgrown track–bed of the long since abandoned main line of the London & South Western Railway from Waterloo to Plymouth and North Cornwall – certainly no sleepy rural branch line. But even though the premier trains of the L & SWR came through the village, their effect was minimal; no more than a brief burst of noise and fury from a pounding steam locomotive. For there never was a station at Sourton and so the village did not experience the feeling of being closer to the outside world that might otherwise have been the case. Nowadays, the peace at Sourton is unbroken save for the traffic on the A386 road, the old L & SWR line from Exeter having been closed beyond Meldon Quarry (where railway ballast is produced) in 1968.

Beyond the railway bridge our path becomes ever steeper until we

Above: Sourton Village Green.

Below: The Sourton Tors from the old railway bridge.

reach a gate that leads out on to the open moor. Here, the stone walls form a 'stroll' (a gap between enclosures, or a funnel-shaped layout to make easier the driving of animals off the moor) and the upward journey relents somewhat as the path swings slowly round towards the Sourton Tors, running more in line with the contours. Along this stretch some curious grassy terraces are to be seen on the right-hand side of the path that bear testimony to, perhaps, one of the most optimistic attempts to extract a profit out of this unforgiving wilderness – an ice works. The terraces are actually the remains of shallow basins into which water was run and then, weather permitting, allowed to freeze: subsequently, the ice was dug out and stored in nearby trenches, before being transported to Plymouth for use in the fishing industry. It may be very exposed on these hills, but the number of days in the year on which the right conditions prevailed for ice making and storage must have been extremely limited and very unpredictable. As a result, it is hardly surprising that the project, started in 1875, lasted for no more than about 10 years.

Some of the remains of the Sourton Ice Works overlooked by Yes Tor.

The track continues past the remains of the ice works and soon levels out. Here, the going is firm underfoot and the turf would not be out of place on the fairway of some genteel Home Counties golf course. An ancient track from Okehampton to Tavistock, called the King Way, runs across this level ground between Corn Ridge on the left and the Sourton Tors on the right, and near where our path crosses it are the remains of an apple crusher. Used in cider-making, this would normally be a circular stone with a trough. The remains here, however, are of a half-stone and leave one to stand and speculate at the frustration that the fracture of the original whole stone must have caused to its maker!

If we walk southwards on our track for about another 900 yards and then strike up the hillside to the east, we will reach what appears to be a

The remains of the granite apple-crusher by the King Way on Sourton Common.

made-up, stony track that comes to a sudden halt. This track is, in fact, the bed of the narrow-gauge railway that ran to the old peat works, which we will reach later at Rattlebrook Head. It began from a junction with the London & South Western Railway at Bridestowe Station and is one of those examples of the incredible lengths to which the promoters of moorland industries were prepared to go. The works, themselves, as we will see, were extensive. In order to take workmen up to the site, and also to bring the peat down efficiently, a railway was laid along a tortuous route that wound around the hills for a distance of 4½ miles, clawing its way up a series of gradients and attaining a total height of 1,100 feet above that of the main railway line. The terrain was a soul-destroying combination of hard rock and soft bog, and the point that we have reached, where the track-bed appears to stop, was, in fact, a shunting head which enabled the trainloads of peat to make their way up and down the hill. This was achieved by reversing direction here and carrying on through a nearby junction.

We must now make our way southwards along the track-bed towards the towering rock-piles of Great Links Tor, which looms darkly on the horizon and has, on its summit, the apparent lone figure of a triangulation point set at 1,923 feet above sea-level. The track-bed rises gradually and before long we find ourselves crossing the young River Lyd, hurrying down from its indeterminate source in the blanket bog to the left. It is also here that a path heads off to the left towards the little outcrop known as

The mighty rock-stacks of Great Links Tor, with the triangulation pillar left of centre.

Gren Tor, which is crowned with another of those supposed logan, or rocking, stones that like many others marked on the map would now need superhuman strength to move. Our route, though, lies straight ahead, with Great Links Tor filling more and more of the southern sky as we continue, firmly convinced that the track-bed is a positive luxury to walk compared to the sodden terrain on either side.

Eventually, the track-bed enters a shallow cutting as it swings round to the east and breasts the ridge between Great Links Tor and Woodcock Hill. At the same time its gradient begins to fall away and, as we pass along the causeway taking the track-bed over the valley of the Rattlebrook, so we can see ahead of us the extensive remains of the Rattlebrook Peat Works. Moreover, half a mile to the south, can now be seen the wind-blown, ruinous silhouette of Bleak House, crouching furtively between Green Tor and the Higher and Lower Dunnagoat Tors.

The ruins of Bleak House.

Peat working began in this area during the 1860s with the prime purpose of processing it for fuel in the form of naptha (Shipley Bridge works used the same process). A number of companies tried in vain to make a commercial success of the venture, but these efforts finally ceased in 1930. The West of England Compressed Peat Company was one of the first to operate here, and Bleak House was built to house the site manager. Isolated and weather-battered though this spot is, if it had been in an unspoilt part of the moor there would have been many days in the year when living here would have had its attractions. But the remaining rubble and rusty iron bear silent witness to the fact that, far from being unspoilt, this place was one of the worst eyesores that man has ever brought about on Dartmoor. Above us, on the slopes of Green Tor and Amicombe Hill, the regular depressions of the peat excavations can be clearly seen; although they are now covered with a copious growth of long grass, this acts only as a shroud, and we can still see the shape, if not the features, of the ugliness that lies beneath.

On an overcast, windy day, this place leaves the visitor with a lasting impression of the utmost desolation. It is not somewhere that many people will wish to linger for too long but, fortunately, there are a number of other places fairly close to hand which can provide a much-needed reminder of the beauty of the moor. Having moved on to Bleak House, itself, one can climb up to the Higher and Lower Dunnagoat Tors on the side of the valley and then on to the heights of Great Links Tor from where there are extensive views over Devon and Cornwall, Bodmin Moor being prominent on the western skyline. If time and daylight permit, one could go on down the valley of the Rattlebrook to its confluence with the River Tavy and into Tavy Cleave. This would, perhaps, be the best antidote to any depression that might be lingering after visiting the peat works site. The return journey could then be made along the high ground, from Hare Tor to Sharp Tor, Rattlebrook Hill and Great Links Tor.

Green Tor.

A less arduous route, except for a relatively short distance in the initial stages that involves some quite hard (and careful) walking over the peat workings, is one that encompasses Kitty Tor. In this instance I would recommend first of all walking up to Green Tor and taking a bearing on the flagpole at Kitty Tor (always assuming that it bears no red flag) before setting off because it disappears behind the bulk of the hillside for most of the way. The tor, itself, is remarkable only for the fact that someone should have bothered to give a name to such an insignificant rock-pile. However, we now have, if the weather is clear, a magnificent view down into the valley of the West Okement with the heights of Yes Tor and High Willhays soaring into the skyline above. Directly opposite is the miniature Lints Tor, crowned by its unmistakable rock-tower, while about half a mile to the north is the curious little stump of Stenga Tor, which sits in its own soggy morass high above the river valley and is one of the original marker points on the boundary of the Forest of Dartmoor. Rather than enduring a one and a half mile slog along the top of the ridge to Branscombe's Loaf, it is now preferable to follow the track north-west from Kitty Tor. One can then go north of the boggy ground above Rattlebrook Head and across to Hunt Tor. Recently it was gratifying to see, here, a pair of red grouse whirring away in front of us. From Hunt Tor a good path leads down the hill to Gren Tor, rejoining the old tramway by the River Lyd, and then our steps can be retraced to the village green at Sourton.

We have returned from an interesting walk to a place that is bleak both by name and nature. Can we learn anything more profound from what we have seen? Well, the brooding desolation of Rattlebrook Head is certainly yet another of those deeply impressive scenes in Dartmoor's varied portfolio. But it is also worth seeing because paradoxically, despite its gloomy and rather depressing spectacle, it gives us cause for optimism that, with care and watchfulness by us all, Dartmoor will remain an unspoilt wilderness unblemished by commercialism. For here is further proof that exploitation for profit does not work on the moor. Look at all the enterprises that have germinated in vain over the centuries; there have been tin mines, peat works, railways, china clay works, the ice works, numerous quarries and plans to enclose vast tracts of land for agriculture. But all, with a few exceptions such as the Lee Moor China Clay Works, Meldon Quarry (both on the moor's edge) and Merrivale Quarry, have sprouted, bloomed briefly, withered and died. The Princetown railway has been closed for 40 years. We hear a lot of concerns expressed by present-day conservationists about the future of the moor, but it must be more unspoilt now than at any time in the last 150 years or so. It has survived through a period when people would tolerate almost any form of industrial development, uncaring or unaware of environmental damage. Surely from now on, with people at large more educated and politicised than at any other time, Dartmoor's future is more secure than ever before.

✳✳✳✳✳

8

AUNE HEAD MIRE

On Dartmoor, it is the peculiar arrangement of the natural features – the tors, valleys and streams – that gives the moor its unique primeval beauty. Scattered on this backcloth are the remains, some relatively recent, others extremely ancient, of man's attempts to live and work in this alien landscape. It would take a lifetime to become familiar with the moor in its entirety: quite apart from topographical detail, a single place can offer an almost infinite variety of impressions; dawn or dusk, summer green or winter white, heavy silence or lashing gale, horsefly heat or numbing cold. In fact, there are places on the moor where the physical features of the landscape are as nothing compared to the mood which it can inspire. I am thinking not of some picturesque waterfall or massive tor, but of another moorland landscape, that of the grassy plateau and tremulous mire found in the highest or remotest parts. Such places tend to be the least visited, not so much because of their distance from civilisation, but due more to the sheer effort and perseverance needed to get across them. Often little of interest is to be seen there – I am thinking now of places like Amicombe Hill, Cowsic Head, Tavy Head, Langcombe Hill, Crane Hill and Nakers Hill. Many books about walking on Dartmoor tend to treat them as areas to avoid, along with numerous mires and bogs, quoting the old adage that 'on Dartmoor the shortest route is seldom the quickest'. Yet, because of their very nature – wild, bleak, featureless and hard to cross – these are places that really should be visited so as to experience the real solitude of the moor and perhaps, at the same time, to find something out about oneself. True, they are not places that you would want to visit too often; but if you do not, your set of Dartmoor experiences will be seriously incomplete.

Everyone will, of course, have individual limits for what he or she is prepared to try, according to health, fitness and confidence. But to go out to, and cross, Tavy Head, for example, is likely to be a memorable experience. You will return with a vivid impression of just how far removed from civilisation the central parts of the moor are, and how difficult they sometimes are to cross. There will be nothing there but a sea of long grass blown into rolling waves by a stiff breeze. Worse still, wading through it, the irregular surface trips and pulls the feet; soon the mind baulks at every step, unsure of what the next foot forward will find. Legs soon become very weary and there is certainly none of the comfort that comes from finding a firm path; any apparent trail is more likely to be a peat cut leading through the hags to nowhere except a soggy morass. Not another soul can be seen; for all the signs that are here, the human race might never have existed. This is another world; the world which was here long before man was created. This is remotest Dartmoor.

To walk to places such as these is to go expecting at least one wet foot. To navigate successfully here is to use the compass regularly and the eyes all the time as the gradual, featureless terrain can be savagely deceptive. At the start of this book I have given some detailed advice about footwear, clothing and other precautions to follow on the moor. But I will stress here that anyone walking in these high, flat areas will find it essential to use a compass in order to navigate, even in clear conditions. Often, there are no landmarks visible other than a larger than average tussock of grass. Even then, unless the compass is regularly checked, you may look up and suddenly find that the large tussock on the skyline has disappeared, leaving nothing by which to navigate. If you have been walking in a straight line, that might not matter; but if you have not, and the mist comes down, the consequences could be serious indeed.

I have described in the chapter on Fur Tor our first experience of the real Dartmoor wilderness. Probably in common with many other moorland walkers, this experience was gained by accident rather than by design – we simply were unaware of what we were letting ourselves in for. It seemed fearfully arduous at the time, but it left a raw and indelible picture of the primeval solitude that exists just a few miles over those hills. In a crowded, modern, creature-comforted way of life this was a new experience, entirely alien to anything we had undergone previously.

Let us now set out to explore one of these 'no-go areas' in the interior fastness of the moor. Aune Head Mire, on southern Dartmoor, is not as featureless as Tavy Head, but it is awkward to reach and, apart from one or two places near its edge, it is impossible to cross. As its name implies, it lies at the head of the River Avon (or Aune), and in a shallow depression that is much less dramatic and extensive than that of Fox Tor Mire. There is also not the same easy path around its rim, and you are likely to see even fewer people in the immediate area.

Combestone Tor, above Hexworthy, is a convenient spot at which to park for the journey. A path runs southwards to Horns Cross, and from this, a deviation should be made on a bearing of 209 degrees. This leads up the slope and, as we level out on the fairly firm ground of Holne Ridge, the titanic bulk of Ryder's Hill looms ahead of us, dominating the

Above: Combestone Tor.
Below: Horn's Cross.

southern skyline. We must head directly for its summit, the highest point on the southern moor at 1,692 feet above sea-level. Its altitude and prominence made it an obvious marker point when the boundary of the Forest of Dartmoor was first delineated in 1240; at that time it was known as Battyshull. From the summit, on a clear day, the view is stupendous. To the north, beyond the Dart Valley, the high wastes of northern Dartmoor dominate. But the most riveting view is away to the south-east, beyond the moor's edge and over the foothills and warmer pastures of lowland Devon to where the River Teign flows into the sea. It is said that sometimes even Portland, some 63 miles away to the east, can be seen from here. Although I have not yet been that fortunate, the thought, nevertheless, makes me feel strangely near to home whenever I am up on Ryder's Hill. That is because, from a prominent hill on the South Downs (close to where I live), I can see across to St. Boniface Down on the Isle of Wight; and from St. Boniface Down, I have seen Portland, which, as I have said is, itself, visible from Ryder's Hill. Three scans to the horizon separate home from the moor – perhaps it is not so far away after all!

Boundstones on the summit of Ryder's Hill. The 'H' stone (a replacement) is called 'Petre-on-the-Mount' and the 'B' stone is Petre's Bound Stone. In the distance can be seen Red Lake spoil tip.

Aune Head Mire lies at the foot of the long slope that falls away to the west of Ryder's Hill. Rather than go directly there, I suggest we head south-westwards towards Fishlake Mire, a mile further down the Avon Valley, and then work our way back up to Aune Head. As we set off, our eyes will be drawn by the conical profile of Red Lake spoil tip, which looms in the distance. The going on this slope is generally fairly rough, with the odd soft spot. I do, however, remember one recent autumn when so much rain fell that the thick grass covering this slope was underlain by one huge sheet of water flowing steadily down the hill into the Avon.

By now, it is very probable that you will not be able to see a single human figure within this vast, hidden, upland valley. All along the sky-line are round, green, wet hills. Lower down, the ground levels out, and beds of rushes festoon the large areas of bog and mire that lie on either side of the river. Near us now is Fishlake Mire, which spreads westwards from the river to lap against the slopes of Green Hill. A tinner's hut can be seen at its edge, keeping fairly close company with a similar set of remains on the east bank of the river. Away to the south, to one side of Huntingdon Warren, is another area of marsh called Ryder's Mire. There

The ruins of the tinner's hut on the edge of Fishlake Mire, with Green Hill and Nakers Hill beyond.

our boys once came gleefully across the rotting corpse of a fully-grown, fully-dead cow; the yellowing bones and horns protruded through the drying blackened hide, which in places had been torn away by foxes to reveal the seething insides. It was, somehow, a fitting symbol of the ever-present threat posed by the moor to the unwary. As we walked away, two ravens circled patiently nearby, waiting for the opportunity to resume their gorging.

This apparently barren and lifeless place can be surprisingly

Many grazing animals on Dartmoor share the fate of this cow, whose skeleton was photographed on the edge of Aune Head Mire.

interesting as far as wildlife is concerned. We once flushed out a pair of red grouse on the slopes of Ryder's Hill and, nearer the river on the same day, we spotted a ring-ousel. Often a solitary heron will be seen flapping languidly along the river.

Above Fishlake Mire, the contours crowd in against the river on either side, preventing the formation of boggy areas, and this allows an easy crossing to be made on the boulders littering the river bed. Above the slopes to the west is the flat, amorphous mass of Nakers Hill, the very epitome of a Dartmoor no-man's-land. Our path lies along the foot of its slopes, following the River Avon upstream along its true right bank. On our left we will see the remains of a tin mine gashed into the hillside, and soon the valley widens out to the west. A green bowl is formed, entrapping the rain falling on the slopes and sending it down to the quaking fen occupying every inch of the flat valley floor to our right. We have arrived at Aune Head Mire.

Patches of water reveal the treacherous ground of Aune Head Mire.

It is like a scaled-down version of Fox Tor Mire, which we visited earlier in the book. Each resembles a rough rectangle of natural sponge, which collects the water from the hills and allows it to run slowly away as a nascent river. Each grudgingly pours its water away through a narrow-necked valley, like the lip of a huge, natural jug. Each is nigh on impossible to cross on foot, except after a prolonged spell of dry weather. Any attempt to 'short cut' across one corner of the mire is likely to result in soaking wet feet and trousers. At best, the ground will just support one's weight, surging up and down in quakes as one stumbles on, riding the ground like a rodeo.

Places like this may lack soaring slopes crowned by a rocky tor. They may be devoid of steep-sided river valleys carved deep into the rock. But wildernesses like Aune Head Mire are dramatic by their brooding emptiness, their uncompromising intolerance to man and their desolate setting in a circle of sombre hills. This is a primitive landscape which ignores human efforts to tame it, not prepared to yield to the demands of civilisation. Here, one must come to feel the forbidding dominance of the landscape, to realise that a safe return depends on one's own resourcefulness and thereby to experience the true nature of the moor.

The return journey lies in a direction over the ridge to the north, but to get there we must first make our way round the mire on its west side and then climb up the slope of Skir Hill. Keeping slightly east of north, we reach the summit. If conditions are clear, we could choose to head down Skir Gut (or Gert), an old tin mine, and follow the stream north. We could then cut across past The Henroost Tin Mine to join the O Brook. Alternatively, we could go directly to the head of the O Brook and follow it down past the remains of Hooten Wheals Tin Mine. In either case, once we have reached the O Brook we should stay on its right, or eastern, bank. We must then cross Dry Lake, which comes down from the right, and keep a look-out for the spot where the Holne Moor Leat comes away from the brook. Here, we should climb eastwards up the slopes above Holne Moor Leat and then cross the dry remains of the Wheal Emma Leat, which has already been mentioned in the chapter about Fox Tor Mire.

For some time now, we have been able to see ahead of us the rocks of Combestone Tor, where we parked several hours ago. These we reach easily by following the contours above the Wheal Emma Leat and arrive back, if not at civilisation, then at least next to a metalled road and probably in the company of others who have parked to enjoy a walk, or the view over the Dart Valley. Not many of them will have been out to Aune Head Mire though, perhaps having been deterred by its distance, remoteness or featureless nature. But for us, having persevered in the long, wet journey out to it, and around its perimeter, there is the sublime feeling of being privy to the secrets of one of the innermost sanctums of Dartmoor.

9

LINTS TOR

The earliest recorded military activity on Dartmoor took place in the early 19th century. At that time there was believed to be a high risk of an invasion by Napoleon and a body of troops was posted to Hemerdon Ball, which is near Plympton and just outside the National Park boundary. Thereafter, throughout the remainder of the 19th century, the use of the moor for seasonal military camping and manoeuvres gradually increased and, in August 1873, large-scale exercises were carried out there for the first time. By all accounts Dartmoor threw everything in its armoury – mud, rain, wind, storms and fog – at the invading armies of some 12,000 men and emerged the winner: the exercise was an unmitigated disaster with wagons becoming embedded in mud, troops getting wet through and camps turning into quagmires. The only indelible impression made was upon the individual and collective psyche of those taking part. They learned the hard way that Dartmoor should never be taken for granted. The military authorities were not, however, deterred for long. In 1876, artillery practice was first carried out on the moor near Okehampton and must have proved successful because it became a regular event. Furthermore, shortly afterwards a permanent camp was established on the moor for use by artillery units while they underwent training.

World War II brought about even more widespread use of the moor for military training and, after hostilities had ceased, some 75,000 acres were retained for training purposes. In 1973, this area was reduced to around 33,000 acres, at which size it remains today. There are three ranges where live firing takes place, all on the northern moor; these are at Okehampton (the largest), Merrivale and Willsworthy (the smallest), and they extend over some of the remotest parts of Dartmoor.

The question of live firing, with its accompanying necessity of temporarily closing the firing area to the public, is one which can arouse strong passions on either side of the debate. Ramblers demand the right to roam wherever and whenever they wish and conservationists decry the effects of firing and military training on the wildlife of the high moor. On the other hand, some people, apart from the military themselves, recognise the need for soldiers to have somewhere to train where the conditions are akin to what they might have to face in the theatre of war. Dartmoor is certainly able to provide these conditions for a large part of the year.

My own view is that the use of Dartmoor for training soldiers is, overall, to the moor's benefit, if only because it places restrictions on access to the moor and helps to preserve it as it is. This may seem perverse, but I question whether the various authorities with their fingers in the Dartmoor pie would be able to resist creating some new 'management scheme' for the northern moor, if it were ever vacated by the army. Already we have the appearance on the O.S. walker's map of something called the 'Tarka Trail'. From the lowland to the north, this leads up to Taw Head by way of the East Okement and Cranmere Pool, before leaving the moor down the River Taw. Yes, Tarka the Otter may have come this way in Henry Williamson's magnificent work of fiction. But to pander to the demands of tourism by creating the 'Tarka Trail' and marking it on the map is, in my view, a contrived and wholly inappropriate intrusion. It is a 'thin end of the wedge' idea that raises concerns about what might replace army activity on the northern moor. What developments might result? The improvement of the military road to give easy access to some Tarka Visitors' Centre on the site of Observation Post 15? I don't believe that this is as far-fetched as it sounds, and my firm view is that the presence of the military is a classic case of 'better the devil you know'.

I am all in favour of large parts of the remote areas of the moor being regularly inaccessible to walkers. It keeps us all off the moor for many days in the year and stops us taking it for granted. Those of us who really want to go out to these particular areas can find out when this is possible by ringing the appropriate telephone numbers listed in the Introduction or by reading the local press. The firing must also help to deter many casual visitors from walking out on to the northern moor at all. This, in itself, helps to limit the disturbance caused by walkers to the moorland wildlife, such as the golden plovers that nest in the area of Cut Hill in early summer. As far as wildlife and the military are concerned, the Ministry of Defence and the Dartmoor National Park Authority liaise regularly over conservation matters to restrict the impact of training on the moorland ecology as far as possible.

I would not want to see the firing areas, or the period they are in use, extended beyond the current limits, and I do wish the soldiers would clear up all their blank cartridges, both expended and still live, after they have finished their day's training. My wife and I once stopped on Ger Tor with our boys, and watched as they cheerfully assembled a Rambo-style ammunition belt, knocking umpteen cartridge cases that they had found into sets of ammunition clips. It was only when we got home that I found that about half a dozen of these cartridges were still live;

although they were blanks, they could still have caused serious injury or death if they had detonated while being knocked into the clips with pieces of rock. Next day they were flung far out into the deep, low tide mud of a harbour near our home, all of us having learned the valuable lesson not to pick up military litter ever again.

Whenever we have met soldiers on exercise on the moor, they are reasonably friendly. But they often seem bemused that civilians should tramp, voluntarily, in all weathers across this wild terrain where they themselves are forced to undergo sometimes severe tests of their personal endurance. These tests are not always orthodox. We once watched fascinated from some way off as two soldiers, some half a mile apart, ran between the red and white poles which mark the firing range boundary on the slopes of Beardown Tor. They were stopping at each pole and doing something to it for about two minutes, before running on to the next one. It was not until we got closer that we realised that one had a pot of red paint and a brush, while the other had a pot of white paint and a brush. They were, in fact, re-painting the alternate colours on the poles. The frantic way in which they were going about this suggested that they had committed some misdemeanour and were reaping the returns for it. Only the Army could concoct such a punishment, and we marvelled at the depth of imagination shown by the sergeant-major who had dreamt up this particular retribution. We did not have the courage to point out to the soldiers that the paint was running in places – perhaps if they had been a couple of miles apart the red paint would have had more chance to dry before the man with the white paint turned up!

The walk out to Lints Tor and back takes us into the Okehampton Firing Range, so it will be necessary to check in advance that there will be no firing on the day of our visit. There is a car park next to the Meldon Reservoir dam, and this is a convenient place from which to set out. Nearby is the huge Meldon Quarry from where the ballast for railway lines throughout the country is extracted and transported away on the truncated line of the former London & South Western Railway from Exeter. The quarry, opened in 1895, can produce some 2,000 tons of ballast each day and is estimated to have reserves sufficient to last between one and two hundred more years. The native rock is hornfels, which is sandstone that has been metamorphosed into rock of a different nature by great heat and pressure.

We set out along the path that leads over the crest of the dam where, perhaps, we may care to pause, either to admire the scale of the engineering work or else to regret the partial drowning of a deep and spectacular valley, depending on one's point of view. Whatever, the reservoir does have its own special beauty on a sunny day, a flat blue mirror set against the lofty backcloth of Corn Ridge and Yes Tor.

Our track, marked on the O.S. 1:25,000 walker's map, avoids a direct

Meldon Reservoir.

onslaught on the slopes of Longstone Hill and, instead, winds up to the top of the ridge. Once we have reached the summit levels, Black Tor appears over a mile away to the south, looming darkly out of the immense rock-strewn hillside that soars up from the West Okement Valley. As we approach it, the slope to our right steepens and we can gaze down into the valley where the West Okement River hurries along the floor, slowing occasionally to indulge itself in a meander. Directly below us, and partially hidden by the hillside, are the elderly, stunted trees of Black-a-Tor Copse, one of three ribbons of upland oaks which cling contortedly to life in the deep river valleys of the moor: the others are Piles Copse in the Erme Valley and, more famously, Wistman's Wood in the West Dart Valley, north of Two Bridges.

As we walk along the slope, Fordsland Ledge dominates the skyline above us, completely obscuring the yet higher ground above, while, opposite, Stenga Tor sits beset by bog on the slopes of Amicombe Hill – that huge monolith of grass-bound granite which stretches southwards from Corn Ridge for over 4 miles to the River Tavy. From Stenga Tor, a well-defined path that marks the boundary of the Forest of Dartmoor leads down into the valley and then across the West Okement at Sandy Ford, which we can see below us – looking sandy! By now, we will also be able to see the distinctive shape of Lints Tor ahead of us. Nearing it, we will be struck by the contrast that it presents with the surrounding landscape. It is almost as if the force that created the moor suddenly tired of massive tors, high rounded hills and deep valleys and decided, instead, to form a delicate miniature of all the grand works that had gone before. The symmetrical slopes of this little hill are crowned by a rock-turret which, once seen, is instantly recognisable whenever one catches sight of it from near or far across the central wastes of the northern moor. To reach its summit, we have to drop into the valley of the Lints Tor Brook, which curls around its slopes and gathers water from the rivulets that descend from Dinger Tor, another of those pimple-like rock-stacks that rear, every so often, from a much greater mass of moorland granite. Then, when we do reach its summit, we can at last stop to rest, refresh and take in the beauty and solitude of our surroundings.

Many books about Dartmoor seem to cover walks past, but never to, Lints Tor. This is a pity for it offers its own special prospect on the northern moor. Compared to the grandeur of its neighbouring tors and hills, it is of a scale that is at once more meaningful and easier to come to terms with. The impact comes from the views to the north and to the south. Northwards, we look straight down the valley of the West Okement to the 'in-country' beyond and realise that it offers the outside world a window into the fastness of Dartmoor: southwards, lie Amicombe Hill and Great Kneeset, while the distant skyline is crowned by the regal rock-stack of Fur Tor. To me, though, the finest aspect is of the subtle, rounded profiles of the little combes above the West Okement. These lie set into the side of Great Kneeset, their shape picked out by delicate shadow, and they look for all the world like the handiwork of some sculptor of infinite patience and care, for whom the sweeping flat grasslands of the moor are a favourite raw material.

'Don't fuss, Dad'. The author's sons ignore all entreaties to take care on Lints Tor.

Before departing it is tempting to climb up on to the top of the little rock-tower on Lints Tor. But be warned, the last time that I attempted

Two views from Lints Tor. *Above:* Looking northwards down the valley of the West Okement, with Corn Ridge to the left and Black Tor to the right. *Below:* Looking southwards towards Fur Tor, with Broad Amicombe Hole to the right.

this a sudden gust of wind hit me on reaching the summit and I almost stepped back off the edge. A far better idea is to continue looking around and admiring the scenery, which also includes, to the east, an unusual view of Okement Hill, from where we might catch the glint of a car windscreen, whose owner has chosen to make the pilgrimage to Cranmere Pool by the short route. Nearer to hand, on the west and east sides, can be seen the steep slopes of the West Okement Valley sweeping aloft to Corn Ridge and High Willhays, sprinkled liberally with a moorland seasoning of grey boulders.

Once we have taken in all we can of the delights of this spot, it is time to move on and head for the heights of High Willhays. At 2,039 feet above sea-level, this is the highest point in England south of the Peak District. It is a bit of a slog for there is no real alternative but to go down into the valley of the Lints Tor Brook and then directly up the hillside to Dinger Tor. This is a route that I would prefer not to describe in detail, except to say that it is one of those endurance tests which sometimes has to be faced on the moor! On gaining Dinger Tor, we can take the much gentler slope to High Willhays, a mile away to the north.

High Willhays summit cairn – and an argument over who has the last chocolate biscuit!

High Willhays does not, in its appearance, live up to its status as the highest point in southern England. It is only 11 feet higher than Yes Tor, whose stark, prominent pinnacles can be seen half a mile beyond. The view over North Devon from this lofty ridge is, however, breathtaking; so, quite often, is the strength of the wind which howls around the exposed ears of anyone walking here. The extensive areas of clittered hillside to be found on the north moor, from this ridge across to East Mill Tor, West Mill Tor and beyond, are readily apparent on a clear day.

Moving on to Yes Tor, we catch a glimpse of Meldon Reservoir far below, between the folds of Longstone Hill and Homerton Hill. We may want to linger here for a long while, unwilling to begin the long and anti-climactic descent. Eventually, though, we will have to face the reality that our journey is nearly over and, perhaps encouraged by the sight of the distant Little Chef restaurant next to the A30 at Sourton, we continue on our way.

Although we have been walking through part of the Okehampton Firing Range, we will not really have noticed any adverse effect from the army activity on the landscape, barring, perhaps, the slender flagpoles at the summit of Yes Tor and on Fordsland Ledge. Further east, however, there are a number of tracks laid down for military vehicles which do rather give away the extensive activity that takes place up here when the range is in use.

The rock-pile of Yes Tor, complete with triangulation point and range flagpole.

Descent is often as hard on the knees as the ascent is on the leg muscles. We will be feeling weary when, at last, we cross the Meldon Reservoir dam again and return to our car. Nevertheless, we should reflect that in our visit today, we have experienced some of Dartmoor's contrast. We have seen the fine, seemingly hand-crafted delicacy of Lints Tor and the grassy combes in the shelter of the West Okement Valley. These subtle features are set down at the foot of the savage, wind-racked leviathans of High Willhays and Yes Tor, which soar skywards on a scale beyond all human comprehension.

❋❋❋❋❋

10

CRANMERE POOL

Cranmere Pool, on northern Dartmoor, is famous not only for its remoteness and being difficult to find, but also for being the first place, by 40 years, to have a Dartmoor letterbox; an idea originated, in 1854, by James Perrott of Chagford. He was the first guide to Dartmoor, and took it upon himself to build, at Cranmere Pool, a modest cairn in which he placed a bottle so that visitors could leave their cards. Evidently something of an entrepreneur, he conducted tourists out to this remote spot: they would be taken as far as Teignhead Farm by horse and carriage and would then proceed the rest of the way on foot, passing over Whitehorse Hill and down on to the central northern morass. Perrott is also known to have taken some famous people out to Cranmere, including Charles Kingsley and R. D. Blackmore, the author of *Lorna Doone*. He died in 1895 at the age of 80, but by then he had already passed his guide's mantle on to his four sons who continued the tradition, but with one or two enhancements. These included the provision, by Mrs Brock of Teignhead Farm, of tea to weary visitors returning from the wilderness, before they headed, horse-drawn, back to civilisation.

The letterbox at Cranmere Pool remained as the only one for many years. In 1894, however, a second box was set up on Belstone Tor, and, in 1938, a third box was established at Ducks Pool in memory of William Crossing, the well-known Dartmoor writer. Others subsequently sprang up at Taw Marsh, Fur Tor, Fishlake Mire and elsewhere until, by the mid-1970s, there were 15 known letterboxes on the moor. By that time, the practice was long-established of leaving a rubber stamp in the letterboxes so that visitors could place an imprint of it on a stamped, addressed postcard, which would then be left in the box for the next visitor to post at a proper Post Office letter box.

Over the next few years there was an explosion in the number of moorland letterboxes and, eventually, a club was formed to provide some form of organisation to what had become a Dartmoor sport. To join, the only requirement was proof that one had found 100 letterboxes, and this still applies, but all letterboxers are now expected to abide by various Codes of Conduct that have been established, both for letterbox owners and letterbox hunters alike. Primarily, these include avoiding private land, not disturbing archaeological remains, walls or buildings (ruinous or otherwise), and following the Country Code. It is also a requirement that letterboxes are not cemented or otherwise fixed into position, unlike the two long-established boxes at Cranmere Pool and Ducks Pool.

Nowadays, a typical Dartmoor letterbox consists of an industrial medical pill canister containing a visitors' book and a rubber stamp, although until recently, when it was considered that they posed too much of a risk of being confused with unexploded military hardware, ammunition boxes were an even more popular form of container. In either event they can, at times, be extremely difficult to locate with hiding places ranging from rock outcrops to peat hags, or simply under a boulder. Altogether, well over 20,000 letterboxes have been registered with the Dartmoor Letterbox 100 Club, but many of them have gradually disappeared, most removed by their owners at different times or, in some instances, vandalised. Nevertheless, at any given time there are still an estimated 3,000 letterboxes on the moor so it is, perhaps, hardly surprising that the old tradition of leaving a stamped, addressed postcard behind has largely disappeared. Rather, the 'modern' letterboxer, on finding a letterbox, merely takes an impression of the stamp in a book (or on whatever else may suit individual tastes), using an ink-pad, and signs into the visitors' book, sometimes by means of a purpose-made, personal, rubber stamp. Quite apart from the enjoyment and satisfaction gained from finding letterboxes at different locations, each member of

Modern-day Dartmoor letterbox paraphernalia – plastic industrial medicinal pill box, visitors' book, rubber stamp and two stones for hiding the 'box' in the enlarged rabbit scrape behind.

the Dartmoor 100 Club also becomes entitled, progressively, to receive more and more cloth badges that denote the total number of letterboxes visited – 100, 200, 500, 1,000, 2,000, 3,000, 4,000 and, finally, 5,000 – and these are often seen displayed prominently (and proudly) on rucksacks.

Letterboxing is a good way to explore the moor, to get some tangible record of the walks one has tackled and to retain the motivation of children on a long walk. Unfortunately, though, quite a number of the letterbox stamps are fairly meaningless, either because of their poor quality or because their subject has no connection whatsoever with the moor. At the same time, however, there are many good quality stamps. Some commemorate, and therefore help to make known, certain Dartmoor legends and traditions, while others may carry a design that is relevant to their location, or just the place-name in lettering. The grandfather of them all, though, is the letterbox at Cranmere Pool. William Crossing, in his *Guide to Dartmoor*, relates that in April 1905 two keen moorland walkers from Plymouth placed a visitors' book in the cairn at Cranmere. During the remainder of that year 609 signatures were recorded, while in 1908 the number was even larger – 1,741. The old visitors' books from Cranmere Pool are kept in Plymouth Library and one records that, on 19th May 1921, the box was visited by the Prince of Wales, later to become King Edward VIII (briefly) and then Duke of Windsor.

One of the motivations of letterboxing is the challenge it presents, but on Dartmoor no challenge is greater to a newcomer to the moor than to find Cranmere Pool. I recall my first visit to it, in the very dry summer of 1982. My wife and I chose what we thought was one of the shorter routes, unaware of the existence of the metalled military road which loops out on to the moor from Okehampton. In retrospect, our ignorance did at least bring home to us its remoteness.

We parked outside the church at Gidleigh, a hamlet buried deep in the tangle of narrow lanes west of Chagford: a lengthy slog up the metalled road past Berrydown, with no moorland in sight, was not the ideal start to this walk. Eventually, though, the gate at Scorhill Farm was reached and we emerged through the stroll on to the open moor. Passing Scorhill Circle, we crossed the Gallaven Brook and the Walla Brook and struck out up the long, slow climb to Watern Tor: it was fortunate that this was a dry summer, otherwise we would soon have been floundering. On arriving at Watern Tor, we realised that this was the place where we must decide either to complete the walk, or, if in doubt because of the weather or the suspicion of a nascent blister, to make a shorter circular route out of what had already been achieved. For between here and Cranmere Pool, a distance of about 2 miles, is some of the most difficult and deceptive terrain on the moor; difficult, because of the deep grass and yet more of my favourite Dartmoor tussocks; deceptive, because even in clear conditions, it is so easy on this vast

Scorhill Circle.

landscape to be misled by eyesight alone into wandering way off course. This is definitely compass territory.

Making our way across the soggy valley of the Walla Brook, we then came to the slopes of the giant whale-back ridge taking in Whitehorse Hill and Hangingstone Hill. Seen from a distance, this would be yet another huge, but rather anonymous rounded hill were it not for the military observation hut crowning Hangingstone Hill. Its tiny, but distinctive, profile perched on top of the hill makes it an instantly recognisable landmark.

From the top of Hangingstone Hill, we had our first, magnificent view westwards over the empty plateau of fen which lies at the heart of the northern moor. Ringing the horizon were some of the great tors of Dartmoor; Yes Tor, High Willhays, Great Links Tor and Hare Tor. Nearer to hand the eye was drawn to Fur Tor, Oke Tor and Steeperton Tor. From the spongy morass which lay directly below us, three major rivers – the East Dart, the Taw and the West Okement – begin their long journeys to the sea as mere trickles through the grass. The peat can hold only so much water, and these streams take with them the excess rain which is hurled across the hills by the Atlantic gales. And somewhere down there was Cranmere Pool – but where? We descended the western slopes to the grassy watershed. I took compass bearings, and soon a comparison with the map told me that we were getting very close. But we wandered for a further half-hour before suddenly coming across a rather bleak depression in the peat hags, featureless except for one very distinctive little stone letterbox – we had found Cranmere Pool! In fact, we had come very close to it 30 minutes before, but, through not going those extra few yards, had missed it completely and had wandered around in a circle. That's how difficult the place is to locate unless you find the upper reaches of the West Okement River and follow it upstream to its head, in which case you can't miss Cranmere Pool.

The letterbox at Cranmere Pool.

Feeling elated, we took several imprints of that famous letterbox stamp and, in time-honoured fashion, left behind a stamped, self-addressed card for the next visitor to post. After a long rest and drink, we consulted our map and set off on the next stage of our circular trip. In the distance we spotted a lone figure coming towards us; as we got nearer, we could see that he was carrying a short butterfly net. Instantly we thought – could this be a modern manifestation of the evil Stapleton of Conan Doyle's *The Hound of the Baskervilles?* In fact, it was not. The figure turned out to be an insect specialist. We asked him if he was looking for Cranmere Pool in a smug tone of voice which implied that, if he was, we, the experts for all of 20 minutes, could give him precise directions. He replied in the negative: he was not looking for Cranmere Pool, but for some unpronounceable insect. His weary tone of voice implied that he had been to Cranmere Pool on many occasions, the novelty had long since worn off and he certainly did not want any guidance in such frivolous pursuits from the likes of us. We finished communicating by tone of voice and bade each other good-bye. As we did so, another horse-fly settled on my arm and dipped its head to sink its teeth (or whatever horse-flies use) into my flesh. Its style was reminiscent of a Harrier jump-jet landing on an aircraft-carrier. I resisted the temptation to call our friend back to ask if he had come across this particular species before, not wanting to receive another subtle put-down. Instead, I put down the horse-fly!

We carried on northwards towards Okement Hill over ground which, had that summer not been so dry, would have given us several wet feet – well, two each. But that day we crossed the dried-up bogs with ease. Suddenly we were astounded to see a caravanette, as incongruous as an ice-cream van in the Sahara, driving slowly into view over the brow of the hill. As we arrived there ourselves, we were further amazed to find a metalled road. This, of course, was the military road which loops out on to the moor from Okehampton Camp. But this was our first visit to Dartmoor and we had not appreciated that it existed, simply because it was not marked in yellow on our O.S. 1:50,000 map. Yes, I am ashamed to admit that we were using this highly inappropriate scale of map instead of a proper O.S. 1:25,000 scale walker's map!

From the road, we doubled back on ourselves, following the track south-eastwards away from the observation post on the military road. By now, the sun was beating down from a cloudless blue sky and there was barely a breath of wind. Our bottles of lemonade were running low. Although we were longing for a quenching drink, we chose too late to conserve what little remained, being unsure of how long and arduous the return journey was going to be. Soon a film of fine, grey dust had gathered on the toe caps of our boots. We pounded along with the vast expanse of the moor shimmering all around us in the still heat of high summer. Such were our first experiences of walking in the heart of Dartmoor. It was only later that I came to realise that these conditions were highly untypical; I have learned the hard way that up here the words dryness, stillness and shimmering heat are rarely applicable.

The track swung to the north-east and soon we were crossing the young River Taw at a ford. Then we took a left turn to the north, passing another observation post. The track was taking its toll on our feet and it was with relief that we left it behind and struck out towards Steeperton Brook, crossing it near the remains of an old tinner's hut. It was then a matter of forcing the mind to over-rule the protests coming from our aching limbs as, by now out of drink, we skirted Hound Tor and followed the valley between Kennon Hill and Rival Tor. Finally, leaving Buttern Hill behind, we began the long descent off the moor. Arriving at the gate at Creaber, we passed through a farmyard where a wonderfully haphazard flock of chickens, ducks and geese pecked contentedly on the dry ground around our feet. The scene would have made the perfect setting for one of those idyllic pictures in an old-fashioned children's storybook.

Soon the metalled road to Gidleigh was beating a painful rhythm on the soles of our feet. But after half a mile, our ordeal was over, as we turned down to Gidleigh Church and collapsed into the seats of the car.

We had learned our first lesson of moorland walking, to carry enough food and drink to last the whole journey, not just half of it, and to take some spare for emergencies.

Now that was getting to Cranmere the hard way. It brought home to us how remote the place is, and it was particularly satisfying to have walked there and back from the edge of the moor. Other epic walks offer themselves to the hardy explorer; up the West Okement Valley from Meldon Reservoir, or up the East Dart from Postbridge, to name but two. Reluctant though I am to encourage the driving of a car out on to the moor along the military road from Okehampton Camp, thereby detracting from the unspoilt emptiness of the place, there is no doubt that this offers an easier, albeit less satisfying way to reach Cranmere. For anyone unable to walk long distances, it is the only way that they will get there at all. For the fit person, use of the road allows all one's energy and time to be devoted to exploring the central wastes, rather than having to make a long outward and return journey. So, if like me, you are prepared, occasionally, to sacrifice a few purist ideals and want to get to Cranmere the easy way, then drive out to the southern end of the loop road and park by the observation post. If you want to get wet

Observation Post 15 on Okement Hill, at the southern end of the military ring road.

feet and tired legs, then take a compass-bearing and follow a straight-line course. Assuming that you don't, then follow the rough track south-eastwards from the observation post along Okement Hill. Shortly before the track begins to swing round to the north-east, you should take a track which leads off to the right towards the pool known as Ockerton Court. Passing the pool on the left, and following the peat pass, the ground begins to fall to the west: a little cleft in the contours, which carries the infant West Okement River, can be seen away to the south. It

Ockerton Court.

is now a matter of heading due south, remaining at the same height along the hillside. In just over half a mile you will reach the West Okement and should now follow it up to its head. As you do so, you will arrive at Cranmere Pool.

You will find that it is just a depression in the peat, whose blackened sides are exposed all around. There is no pool; it is believed to have been drained of its water by shepherds in the early 19th century. Cranmere; the name comes from the crane, or heron, sometimes to be seen by a moorland stream. So, you ask, why all the fuss about this rather soggy, anonymous bowl in the ground? To this I answer, it is not what the place is, but what it represents – a focal point in the green fastness which stretches away in all directions as far as the eye can see. In a landscape of gigantic hills and vast distances, over-arched by a huge sky, it is a place whose scale is at one with man. If you struggled to find it, then you most definitely are not the first to have done so. By taking the effort, and effort it certainly is, to come out here, and perhaps make use of the letterbox, you are performing an act beyond worth. You are maintaining a Dartmoor tradition, one begun many generations ago by James Perrott, an archetypal moorman. Like those first visitors whom he brought here so long ago, you cast your eyes around to the distant horizons and realise that you have come to a place which, in all this wilderness, is the most remote of all.

✳✳✳✳✳

11

BEARDOWN MAN

No-one with even brief experience of walking on Dartmoor can fail to have become aware at some time of the traces of early man. Hut circles, stone circles, standing stones, stone rows and kistvaens are still to be seen scattered across the face of the moor, bearing mute witness to the passing of thousands of years. They have remained while countless generations have come and gone: they have lasted for a period of time that is impossible for a human being to gauge, but is barely the blink of an eyelid in terms of the age of the landscape on which they stand. Yet these stone vestiges and their awesome surroundings both owe their existence to man's inability to live on, and exploit, the moor. Had it proved possible to make money out of Dartmoor's hills, these mysterious monuments would have been swept away long ago; that they still exist today is nothing less than a triumphant celebration of man's failure to conquer Dartmoor.

The prehistoric remains are as pertinent a part of the Dartmoor landscape as the tors and the valleys. A long sweeping slope covered with a random sprinkling of natural boulders is given its own identity by the presence of a stone row. Like a lightship on the open sea, a standing stone on the high grassy uplands provides reassurance and a sense of position to anyone walking there. But there is always a contradiction: the sight of that standing stone may tell you with certainty where you are on the map; however its age and mystery remind you of the uncertainty of your own existence and your infinitesimal importance in human history.

At the time when the hut circles were roofed and were home to our ancestors, the climate that prevailed on Dartmoor was somewhat kinder than it is today. Even so, it was no tropical paradise; the hut circles are found predominantly in the shelter of river valleys and not on the exposed hilltops. Particularly noteworthy are the settlements in the valleys of the rivers Tavy, Walkham, Avon, Erme, Yealm and Plym.

The stone circles of Scorhill and the Grey Wethers may be less impressive than Stonehenge, but are equally mysterious in their purpose and presence. More remarkable still, are the stone rows, especially the one which runs for 2 miles southwards from Green Hill on the southern moor.

The standing stones are, perhaps, the strangest of all the ancient remains on the moor. Quite often, like the Longstone on Shovel Down, they are associated with a stone row. But there are others which, keeping their own counsel, stand like solitary sentinels keeping perpetual watch over the immediate surroundings.

One of the more remote standing stones is Beardown Man, near Devil's Tor, high above the valley of the River Cowsic. There are several ways of approaching it, but let us start at Bagga Tor, at the end of the narrow road that winds its way from Peter Tavy up on to the high western slopes of the moor. This road terminates at a gate just short of Bagga Tor, itself, but a car can be parked inside the gate, clear of the track.

This track continues where the metalled road left off. Passing the little rock-pile of Bagga Tor, it heads towards the high ground of Lynch Tor, which looms on the eastern skyline. Within half a mile we pass a military look-out post, which reminds us that we are entering the Merrivale Firing Range (if the red flag is not flying, that is). Then a final gate leads out on to the open moor, and we find ourselves in a wide stroll, whose walls diverge away from us up the slopes of Lynch Tor and Wapsworthy Common. When I was last here, my family and I were overtaken by a farmer on his way to check the well-being of his more far-flung sheep. He was perched on one of those rugged four-wheeled motorcycles, which look so tempting to anyone who has ridden the two-wheeled variety in their youth. They must be an ideal therapy to a one-time teenage motorcyclist in a mid-life crisis!

As the walls of the stroll fall away behind us, we have to decide whether to go to the north or to the south of Lynch Tor, or directly over its summit. For me, there is only one choice; I don't go to Dartmoor to scurry around the lower reaches of the hills! The full impact of this landscape can only be appreciated from its highest, or remotest, points; so

Lynch Tor, with Standon Down beyond.

you go whichever way you want, but I'm going to the top of the tor!

It is a fairly stiff climb, but it is relatively short and does not have to be rushed. On gaining the summit, the reward for the effort is a tremendous view westwards over the pastures of West Devon into Cornwall. Near to hand is the highest point on this hill, Limsboro Cairn, an ancient and prominent marker. In the 1240 perambulation it was chosen by the jury of twelve knights as one of the points defining the position of the Forest boundary. From here, this runs northwards to Western Red Lake, and southwards to White Barrow and Great Mis Tor, whose unmistakable profile dominates the skyline in that direction. But our route lies to the east, behind Lynch Tor and down towards the valley of the River Walkham, a river whose waters begin as a trickle from the windswept uplands of the northern moor and hurry on down through Merrivale and Horrabridge to join the River Tavy at a spot known as Double Waters. Quite soon we meet a track which comes down from the north before turning, abruptly, eastwards towards the river, and this we must now join. It is, in fact, a branch of the old road known as Black Lane (a namesake of the track that leads from the Erme Valley to Fox Tor), which ran from Baggator Gate, along the western slopes of Lynch Tor and out as far as the head of Eastern Red Lake, where there was once an extensive area of peat ties. Consequently, it will come as no great surprise to learn that the track was used as a route for the transportation of peat, something that applies, equally, to the track that we are now following. The difference, however, is that our track catered for the movement of peat from Walkham Head, which was used as fuel for smelting the tin ore at the Wheal Betsy Tin Mine, near Mary Tavy.

At the bottom of the valley the ground is rather soft in places, but

The remains of Black Lane (north) near Lynch Tor.

there is a ford where this branch of Black Lane crosses the river. From the ford, we proceed directly up the long slope ahead of us and soon pass through the substantial set of grassy banks that still remain from the Walkham Head Peat Works. On we go and at last the ground begins to level out as we reach the watershed. We are now on one of those flat, featureless Dartmoor hilltops that is the birthplace of a number of streams and rivers. There are several 'heads' around us; Walkham Head and Cowsic Head are quite near, whilst further on are West Dart Head and Tavy Head. Near at hand, too, are the heads of two feeder streams of the River Tavy. After dry weather, the ground here, seemingly, cannot decide whether to be firm or boggy. Often there is a slight crust, which will take one's weight yet never feels particularly solid under foot.

All the while that we were climbing out of the Walkham Valley we had a good view to the south, but our view to the north was hidden by the high ground to our left. Now, though, we can see over a green land-scape of lunar-like emptiness to the northern skyline, where the rocks of Fur Tor stand squat and immovable in their lonely domain. Between them and us is 1½ miles of the emptiest terrain on the whole moor, where the rough ground can drain the energy from the legs of even the fittest walker. So, let us make our way, instead, to Cowsic Head, which is on the southern side of this vague, amorphous plateau. As we approach it, the ground begins to fall away to form a gentle gully, so typical of a Dartmoor river head. At first no water will be seen but, going lower, we find (or hear) a trickle of water running through the deep grass at our feet. The young stream runs ahead of us and drops over into the deeper valley which we see beyond, but whose floor is hidden from view by the intervening ground. We will stay on the high ground for now and follow the contour along the eastern slope of the Cowsic Valley. We can now see Devil's Tor on the skyline and, just below it, is a solitary pillar of granite occupying a commanding spot overlooking the rapidly deepening river valley below. At last we are approaching Beardown Man.

The 'man' part of its name is thought to be derived from the Celtic word maen, meaning stone. When we reach it, we will be struck by its size; it stands some 11 feet tall and is the largest isolated menhir on the moor. What its purpose was, no-one knows; it could have been an object of potent pagan symbolism for early man or, at the other extreme, an overblown marker post on some long vanished track. Whatever the original reason for its existence, it now serves as useful confirmation of a walker's location, particularly in misty weather. But on a fine day, one need only stand here to appreciate the commanding view. We can then, perhaps, understand how, countless centuries ago, our forebears might have been moved to erect this massive piece of granite, whose mystic presence is entirely at one with its surroundings.

Beardown Man is the one without the flat cap!

When at last it is time to move on, we should aim to cross to the western side of the Cowsic as high up as possible, ideally above the confluence of the three little feeder streams at the upper end of the valley. Having done so, we make our way southwards along the contour and, in just under half a mile, turn westwards up the hill to reach Conies Down Tor. As we breast the ridge, we can look beyond the Cowsic Valley to where, in the far distance, the blue-grey hills of the moor meet the southern sky.

We leave the Cowsic Valley behind and can now see the little Conies Down Water below to our left. Further west, a prominent path disappears over the ridge of Conies Down. This is the Lich Path. Its name, an old word for corpse (also found in lychgate), betrays its origins as a path along which the body of a deceased parishioner would be carried from the outlying parts of Lydford parish for burial in Lydford churchyard. It should be appreciated that Lydford was then an extensive parish stretching from the village, itself, right across the northern moor to Postbridge, Bellever and the settlements such as Babeny in the East Dart Valley. Legend has it that a corpse would be carried along this path over the lonelier parts of the moor, either strapped across a horse or in a horse-litter. On reaching a wood, still known as Coffin Wood, where the Baggator Brook joins the Tavy, the body would then be transferred to a coffin and carried somewhat more reverently to its final resting place at Lydford. It is believed that on the eastern side of the moor there were several branches of this path, each leading from one of the little settlements to the Lich Path proper.

We must now make our way down the gentle slope to join the Lich Path, one of several moorland paths that are marked on the walker's map of Dartmoor in bold green dashes. Prominent they may be on paper, but in reality it can quite often be a different tale when one attempts to follow them. I am thinking now, in particular, of the Abbots' Way where it heads south-eastwards from Nun's Cross Ford, over Hand Hill and down into the Plym Valley, and cannot help wondering whether the name started life as a rose-tinted figment of someone's imagination.

Above: The ford where the Lich Path crosses the River Walkham.

Below: The Lich Path is sunken as it climbs the eastern slopes of Cocks Hill.

On the other hand, the Lich Path, certainly in this part of the moor, is clearly a track that has been used for a very long time indeed. It crosses the River Walkham at a well-defined ford and is positively sunken as it winds its way westwards over Cocks Hill. Walking along it, you appreciate how useful it must have been, in these wild surroundings, to anyone undertaking (no pun intended) the onerous journey across the northern moor. One is also filled with a sense of walking with one's forebears along an ancient trackway that spans both the wilds of the moor and many previous centuries.

We follow the Lich Path over the gradual slopes of Cocks Hill. As we start to drop down into the valley of the Tavy, we pass a grassy mound on our left; this is White Barrow, yet another ancient boundary mark of the Forest of Dartmoor. Ahead, we can see the stroll whose walls funnel into the gate by the military look-out post that we passed at the start of our walk. Reaching this gate, and still on the Lich Path, we retrace our steps of earlier in the day until, half a mile further on, we find ourselves arriving back at our starting point.

Our journey has not only covered a few miles but also thousands of years of man's presence on the moor. After countless centuries of evolution, we cannot begin to comprehend the hardship, cruelty and short-lived existence that was the life of those people of the Neolithic or Bronze Age who erected Beardown Man. We have walked along the Lich Path, a track which our closer forebears used out of bleak necessity, rather than for leisure and relaxation. Their lives were more comfortable than those of their prehistoric ancestors, but they would not have believed how immeasurably the lives of their descendants would improve in comparison to their own. Nevertheless, there is one thing that is surely common to all those generations who have known the moor and those who have yet to do so; and that is a profound sense of wonder at the wild and empty landscape that we have seen before us today.

12

WATERN TOR

This book was conceived as an attempted cure for acute frustration at being unable to walk on Dartmoor. Between November 1994 and March 1995 my family and I were restricted to only a single moorland walk, a short, blustery, damp trek over King's Tor and the Princetown railway track-bed. It was as if there was a conspiracy by the weather to thwart our every attempt to visit Devonshire. Any fine spell of weather during the week seemed to dissolve into rain, or a forecast of rain, at the weekend, making any walking trip to Dartmoor unviable. In fact, I recall one sequence of several weekends when the rain teemed down every Saturday. During that period I eventually decided to counteract the gathering despondency by visiting the moor on paper, being unable to do so in reality: I felt that this was a more positive move than sending hate mail to the BBC weather forecasters!

We had, finally, to wait until 1st April before Providence decreed that a fine day in Devonshire should be forecast to occur on a Saturday, and responded by quickly making up our minds that our destination was to be Watern Tor, another of the boundary markers of the Forest of

The parking spot at Batworthy.

Dartmoor. After an early, bleary-eyed start from home, we arrived at the edge of the moor, above Chagford, at 8.30 a.m. We were heading for our chosen starting point for the walk at Batworthy, which, like many of the access points to north-eastern Dartmoor, is lost at the end of a tortuous, narrow road. After much twisting and turning, we finally drove over the cattle grid on to the open moor where, to our left, Kestor Rock loomed prominently on the hillside. Then, shortly after we had passed the ancient Round Pound on our right, the road dived down into a little valley to terminate at Batworthy.

After 5 months of deprivation, it was uplifting to step out of the car early that April morning and to sense the Dartmoor ambience once again. Batworthy Brook splashed its way among the rocks nearby, and a westerly breeze brought with it that familiar Dartmoor scent – a subtle cocktail of wet grass and sheep. The sun, too, was starting to win its battle to penetrate the clouds that had come with the dawn.

We followed a soggy path towards Batworthy Corner and then took a drier route up the hillside on to Shovel Down. Soon we could see one of the stone rows that are to be found here and, once over the ridge, reached the Longstone. This ancient menhir is one of the markers of the

The Longstone, with Kestor Rock beyond. The inscriptions are 'GP' (Gidleigh Parish) and 'DC' (Duchy of Cornwall).

boundary of the Forest of Dartmoor, which we now followed westwards with Thornworthy Tor and Fernworthy Forest both prominent to the south. Along the way, a man walking his dog called out a warning that

Stone row on Shovel Down.

he had seen the fresh footprints of a big cat over by Fernworthy, which was somewhat disconcerting because it was at that time that reported sightings of pumas and leopards on Bodmin Moor were making national news headlines, under the sensational title of 'The Beast of Bodmin'. Nevertheless, it was the first occasion that we had heard of such a thing on Dartmoor and so, gripping walking sticks harder, we strode on, but in half-relief and half-disappointment we saw nothing apart from the squat bulk of Stone Tor hunched on the hillside ahead of us. We did, however, speculate that if such creatures existed they could easily survive in this part of Dartmoor with plenty of sheep available as a source of food and Fernworthy Forest providing a natural means of shelter.

Whilst on the subject of animals, it is interesting to contrast the demeanour of the three types of animal commonly encountered on Dartmoor. The walker will come across cattle, sheep and ponies all over the moor. Cattle, after eyeing a stranger carefully for a minute or two, will normally resume their grazing unconcerned. I am told, however, that this is not always true if one is accompanied by a dog. If the cattle have calves, they may chase the dog, seeing it as a threat to their off-spring. Indeed, in the first few pages of his *Guide to Dartmoor*, William Crossing tells how, in the mid-1880s, he, his wife and his dog were pursued by bullocks on Ugborough Moor and just made it over a wall in time. He considered that the dog had been the sole source of fury to the cattle, whose demeanour changed for the better as soon as the dog was out of their sight on the other side of the wall.

Ponies generally take little notice of walkers on the moor. They sometimes appear highly strung and can, for no apparent reason, gallop suddenly away. When they do so, there is a strong contrast between their calm grazing and their wild, dramatic elegance as some unseen force sweeps them away together over the hill. The outstanding characteristic of the sheep, on the other hand, is their unwavering and monumental stupidity! One comes across many dead sheep on the moor, some drowned, some jammed under rocks, and others just lying in the open with fleece and bones scattered around. I once found a sheep lying on its back and wedged in the gap between two 6-feet long rocks, each about a foot high. Its legs kicked pathetically in the air as I approached, and it was clearly totally incapable of freeing itself. Grabbing it by the back legs, I was able to release it very easily, upon which it made off without any obvious gesture of gratitude. In fact, the only time that I have noticed any modicum of intelligence in a sheep was when we freed a lamb, which had become stuck in a small gap in a drystone wall. It had apparently been lodged there for some time because its sides were rubbed raw but, whatever, its mother was bleating frantically as we approached, seemingly asking for help. I then responded by loosening a couple of stones from the wall, and as the lamb walked off so the ewe gave a few more bleats, only on this occasion in a different tone that sounded uncannily like relieved gratitude. It was the first and last time that I felt myself to be on the same mental wavelength as a sheep!

Like the animals, the birds that one sees on the moor can also be very interesting. Once, on a walk, one of our boys spotted a strange-looking white bird some 50 yards away. Through the binoculars, its size appeared to be between that of a sparrow and a blackbird, and, after much speculation about its identity, with guesses ranging from a great grey shrike to an albino wheatear, we decided that it was a snow bunting. Later that evening, at home, our bird books confirmed that we had been right. We have found that, on Dartmoor, the occasional rarity will crop up among the more common birds such as buzzards, pipits and wheatears. The most rewarding sighting that I have had on the moor was of a single red kite, which I noticed over Birch Tor whilst driving from Postbridge to Moretonhampstead. It would be nice to think that, one day, these spectacular birds, with their distinctive forked tails, will become as commonplace as the buzzard in Devon. Talking of buzzards, I find it strange that while they are so uncommon in the countryside of Hampshire and West Sussex, in Devon they are frequently to be seen, even in populated areas. In fact, apart from Dartmoor, the place where I most often see buzzards in Devon is alongside the M5 motorway, sometimes perched on the lighting columns.

Returning now to our walk, we duly reached Stone Tor with its adjoining enclosure wall, crossed Langridge, the high ground to the west of Stone Tor Brook, and descended into the valley of the North Teign River. Ahead of us was the steep slope of the ridge which takes in Manga Hill to the south and Watern Tor to the north. To our right we could see where the little stream known as Hew Lake (not 'Hugh' as on the O.S. map) joins the North Teign at Hew Lake Foot. Hundreds of years earlier, in 1240, the perambulators of the Forest of Dartmoor knew this confluence more elaborately as Wotesbrokelakesfote and thought it important enough to be a Forest boundary point.

Having boulder-hopped over the North Teign, we gritted our way up the stiff gradient of the opposite hillside and eventually arrived at the rather undistinguished Manga Rock. From there, we pressed on up the combe of Hew Lake to where the boundary wall of the old Teignhead newtake crowned the skyline and then followed this wall northwards along the ridge until our destination, Watern Tor, could be seen just a short distance away.

The rock-stack of Watern Tor contrasts vividly with the rounded grassy hilltop on which it sits. The climate has ravaged the original rock profile into a smooth ridge blanketed in grass, except, that is, for this stubborn chunk of granite. The foliated rock formation bears witness to

Two views of Watern Tor. *Above:* From the east, with the illusory hole clearly apparent. *Below:* From the west, where the true nature of the rock-pile is revealed.

the extremes of weather which have battered and blasted it over millions of years. There is a 'hole' through the base, with a gap which leads from it to the top of the rock-pile. Indeed, the alternative name for this rock is the Thirlstone (holed stone), a derivation identical to that of the similar rock structure that lies on Thurlestone Sands, near Salcombe. The layered formation of the Thirlstone is normally found only in sedimentary rocks as a result of particles being deposited by settlement under water and being compressed. Granite is, of course, an igneous rock and would not normally have the stratified appearance. However, here it is believed to have been caused by the granite cooling more slowly than usual.

It is hardly surprising that such a distinctive, unambiguous feature should have been chosen in 1240 as a boundary point by the perambulators of the Forest of Dartmoor. From here, the boundary they chose ran northwards to Hound Tor and southwards to Hew Lake Foot. The wild prospect from Watern Tor can have changed little over the intervening centuries. On the April day when we visited it, visibility was good and we could see eastwards to the cultivated land beyond the confines of the high moor. Nearer to hand, though, the emptiness and desolation were profound; to the east, the slopes of the tor fell away to the low-lying ground between the North Teign and the Walla Brook; northwards were Hound Tor and the promontory of Rival Tor; and westwards, beyond the valley of the Walla Brook, lay the great bulk of Hangingstone Hill, which screened from our view the central plateau of the northern moor. Wild Tor could be seen to the north-west. The whole landscape was washed in two-tone brown; the pale colour of dead grass predominated, but was broken here and there by the darker patches of the previous year's bracken. It was striking how these brown shades of the moor contrasted with the distant green of early spring which was already established on the lower, less exposed pasture of South Devon, and this difference in colour demonstrated graphically that here, on the Dartmoor hills, the season of growth and life is so much shorter.

We sat on the rocks of Watern Tor for more than an hour contemplating the solitude of the landscape that lay around us, with no other human figure to be seen. Spring was about to bring renewal to that brown and barren wilderness, and we were glad that our acquaintance with Dartmoor had, itself, been renewed on that sunny April day.

13

THE WHITEBARROWS

Shipley Bridge.

Can it really be true? A few short hours ago I was driving across the Hampshire Downs as dawn approached, but now I am parked next to the River Avon at Shipley Bridge on Dartmoor; all is vibrant and green, yet quiet and serene in the sunlit calm of an early midsummer morning. I sit there for a few minutes, stupefied by an overdose of this miracle drug. Then, two pairs of socks go on, followed by boots, and I go through the mental checklist – wallet, car keys, jumper, map, compasses, whistle, drink and food. Yes, all is packed, and at twenty to eight I'm off on a walk to Eastern and Western Whitebarrow. Not a vast distance, in comparison with my other walks, and I'm not going to the innermost recesses of the southern moor. Instead, I just want to look out over them and, in particular, to stand on Western Whitebarrow and see, today, the view that William Crossing saw from there 100 years ago. He described this in his *Guide to Dartmoor*, pointing out that, from Western Whitebarrow, the valleys of the moor are so aligned that Cosdon Hill can be seen 16 miles away on the northern edge of Dartmoor.

I follow the metalled road northwards alongside the Avon, which gurgles among the rocks to my right. The Avon Valley is verdant with trees in full leaf; the rhododendrons are coming into flower and the slopes are blanketed in a fresh green growth of bracken. I want to get up on to the hilltop to my left and work my way along past Black Tor. So, after a short distance, I leave the valley road and take the branch that leads up the hillside to the Avon Waterworks. At the junction of the roads is the short, square Hunters' Stone bearing the inscription of a number of names, such as Trelawney. These evoke childhood memories of reading *Treasure Island* but are, in fact, the names of well-known local huntsmen of 100 years ago.

The Hunters' Stone.

After a quarter of a mile, as the road enters the waterworks, I strike off northwards towards Black Tor, glad to be on open moorland. Down below is a tree-shrouded enclosure where once stood Brentmoor House: now the only visible indicators of human habitation are the rhododendrons among the trees. Upon reaching the outcrops of Black Tor, I can see ahead of me a long curve of hillside sweeping round the valley to the bracken-shrouded remnants of the Bronze Age settlement known as Ryder's Rings. Following a level course along the contour over the close-cropped turf, I soon reach the settlement and, after passing close by on the higher side, walk along the bed of the now dry Shipley Leat to make sure that I stay more or less at the same level. Down below me, the River Avon splashes its way among the rocks of the valley floor, while to the south the road veers from one bank to the other over a little stone bridge. The most striking view, however, is to the north, where the wall of the Avon Dam has come into view.

The Avon Dam.

This dam holds back many millions of gallons of water for public supply, to form an impounding reservoir. It is allowed to fill with surplus water brought by the burgeoning rainfall of the winter months, but during the summer, when the upstream river flow diminishes, the reservoir level falls as the peak water demands of the Devonshire holiday season are satisfied. Public supplies, as one would expect, are also drawn off throughout the remainder of the year, and a flow sufficient for the ecology of the river is maintained downstream of the dam by adjusting the outlet control valves. Often in the winter, the reservoir will fill completely and water will overtop the crest to descend in spectacular fashion to the river below.

Those bare facts of water engineering say nothing of the conflicting emotions aroused by the sight of the dam and its reservoir. To some, it is an unnatural excrescence which blights the beauty of this upland river valley. But, to me, it lends a peculiar power to the landscape: on the one side is a huge body of deep blue water; on the other a little stream in an empty rocky valley. All that stands between them is that comparatively thin wall of concrete, built in a gentle arch to withstand the colossal forces exerted on it by the water. The soaring heights of the dam, anchored deep in the underlying rock, provide a direct visual measure of the otherwise latent energy of the moor.

It is time now to leave the river valley and to head for the hills above. From the top of Zeal Gulley, I climb on a bearing of 15 degrees out of the valley towards the first of today's destinations, Eastern Whitebarrow, some 300 feet above. The view behind me becomes rapidly more extensive. A patchwork of pasture stretches away to the English Channel in the far distance. To the south, the sea appears bluish-grey, but on the eastern horizon the sun ignites its surface in a dazzling strip of silver. Ahead of me, the slope comes alive in a kaleidoscope of green as the grass ripples in the strengthening breeze ... until the uniform skyline of green meeting blue is suddenly broken by the top of a turret-like drystone pile. Eventually, as I bridge the final crest of the hill, all is revealed when I am confronted by the strange spectacle of the Eastern Whitebarrow cairn. Believed to date from the Bronze Age, it has a profile which strongly resembles that of an early submarine; a streamlined, elliptical heap of granite is crowned by a circular 'conning tower' of stones, which is probably a much later addition to the base pile. From a distance, this otherwise anonymous ridge is given an instant identity by the presence, on its summit, of this curious edifice.

Eastern Whitebarrow.

The view behind me is now forgotten because, at last, I can see what lies beyond the ridge. On the way up, the dominant view was of the rolling carpet of Devonshire pastureland, civilised and fashioned by man over innumerable centuries. But, on reaching the hilltop, the curtain is pulled aside and suddenly there is revealed an entirely different land-scape, one which is untamed and has never bowed under the yoke of the human race. Beneath me now are the empty wastes and innermost recesses of southern Dartmoor.

There is now a feeling of being richly rewarded for my long climb. As

Just two of the magnificent views from Eastern Whitebarrow. *Above:* Looking up the Avon Valley, with the Red Lake spoil tip, North Hessary Tor and Great Mis Tor to its left and with Huntingdon Warren Hill to its right. *Below:* Looking up the valley of the Western Wellabrook; to the left is Huntingdon Warren Hill with Ryder's Hill beyond; in the centre is Snowdon; to the right, on the distant horizon, is Hameldown.

I sit there recovering my breath, so I am able to start taking it all in. To the east, the uniform green of Grippers Hill is broken by a thin, lighter strip that marks the route of the Jobbers' Road (or Abbots' Way) as it comes over the hill to the Avon Reservoir (the reservoir, itself, is hidden from view by the bulky shoulder of the hill at my feet). Further round, I find that I am looking directly along the axis of the hill of Huntingdon Warren, where, on the eastern side, are the enclosure walls and the solitary sycamore tree at the site of Huntingdon Warren House; beyond it are the tin workings at the head of the Western Wellabrook underneath Snowdon and Ryder's Hill. On the western side of the warren, I can see straight up the Avon Valley beyond the rocks of Broad Falls to the spongy morasses of Aune Head Mire. However, the most striking aspect of Huntingdon Warren is of the face of the hill itself. When one is walking around, or over, this hill it is often hard to spot the various remains on its slopes because of one's proximity to them. But now, from this distance, its uniform green bulk is given meaning and definition: the sun picks out in delicate and subtle shadow the outlines of the ancient settlements and the many pillow mounds dating from its days as an active rabbit warren.

Prominent in the middle distance is the dark, menacing cone of the Red Lake spoil tip. When one stands close to it, it looks no more than it really is – a heap of spoil which no-one could be bothered to clear up. But from here, against the anonymous backcloth of Nakers Hill, its appearance is that of a sacred pyramid symbolising the infinite mystery of the wilderness all around it. Nearer to hand, just over half a mile away, is Western Whitebarrow, with its less distinctive cairn. Rather than going directly to it, I decide to drop back on to the slope behind me to explore Petre's Pit, at the head of the Bala Brook. Its position is revealed by a gouge in the hillside several hundred yards away. As I approach it, I find myself crossing the track-bed of the Zeal Tor Tramway, which was once used to convey peat dug from ties near Western Whitebarrow down to the naptha works at Shipley Bridge. In one or two places on the tramway, it is still possible to see the iron spikes that retained the rails.

Petre's Pit is the site of a short-lived china clay works started in 1872. The clay dug here was sent down to Shipley Bridge for settlement and processing, the buildings formerly used for distilling naptha from peat being taken over and used by the clay mining company, which built settling beds on the hillside there. Petre's Pit also bears the tell-tale signs of tin mining activity. The name Petre commemorates Sir William Petre, lord of the manor of Brent, who died in 1571.

I continue the walk by going on up the hill in the shallow valley above Petre's Pit and then veer northwards in order to reach Western Whitebarrow. In doing so, I soon reach the track-bed of the Zeal Tor Tramway once more and follow it until arriving at a point where a group of a dozen or so cattle is grazing. They look up startled as I approach and then stand their ground staring at me. Feeling more than a little disconcerted, I respond by also standing my ground and staring at them, at the same time wondering whether they realise that they could trample me into the ground, without drawing breath. Gripping my walking stick ever tighter, I eventually take a step forward, bang the stick hard against the ground and, finally, the spell is broken; a bullock snorts hard before running off, and the others take their cue from him, thereby leaving me able to continue on up the hill to my next destination.

Western Whitebarrow, looking towards Eastern Whitebarrow.

When I arrive at Western Whitebarrow it is still only mid-day, yet it is also 5½ hours since breakfast in a motorway service station and so the decision is made to have lunch – but first, what is to be seen here? The cairn is fairly nondescript, but still contains the remains of a crude hut. This was built from stones off the cairn by the men who worked on the nearby peat ties that fed the naptha works below. In constructing their hut, they tore up the adjacent Petre's Cross, a 16th century boundary marker for the manor of Brent, broke off its arms and used it as a lintel for the fireplace! After the naptha industry closed down, the hut fell into disrepair and, eventually, the cross (minus arms) was discovered in the ruins and re-erected, upside down, in the cairn. But that 19th century vandalism has reduced this ancient cairn to a sad, meaningless pile of stone. Surely it could quite easily be restored to something like its former appearance? There seems little point in preserving in aspic these demeaning remains, in which the part-cairn, the part-hut and the part-cross stand together like a forlorn bunch of hopeless misfits.

Recently a cross on Ter Hill was found to be deteriorating in the constant freezing and thawing of the Dartmoor climate. It was carefully copied and replaced, thereby enabling a Dartmoor object peculiar to its location to be preserved, albeit not the original relic. Perhaps similar, but

A close-up view of Western Whitebarrow. Note the shaft of the broken cross to the right of the picture.

more ambitious action, is needed in the case of Western Whitebarrow so as to restore it to a semblance of its original shape and meaning. I would not want such a philosophy to extend to the levelling of Red Lake tip or the filling in of Erme Pits. Instead, I am merely suggesting that a 150 year-old wrong should be righted, with careful control and advice along the way. The overall effect on the landscape of the southern moor would be negligible.

Back to today's walk or, perhaps more accurately, my lunch-break – as I sit there on Western Whitebarrow eating contentedly in the sun, it is noticeable that the view north is similar to that from Eastern Whitebarrow. But I can now see down into the Erme Valley, where the dusty white track-bed of the Red Lake Tramway winds sinuously around the nearer slope. In the distance I see North Hessary Tor and Great Mis Tor, while on the far skyline I can just make out the profile of Great Links Tor. How these giants of the moor are made to seem puny by their vast distance away! And yes, just as William Crossing saw and wrote, there on the horizon, north of north-east, the hills part to reveal the rounded shape of Cosdon Hill, far away on the northern edge of Dartmoor. My line of sight to Cosdon passes over Aune Head Mire, Skir Hill, Hexworthy Mine, Dunnabridge Pound, The Sheepfold, the western edge of Fernworthy Forest, the valley of the North Teign River, Hew Lake Foot, Ruelake Pit and on to Cosdon, itself, 16 miles away.

Eventually, I decide to head back down the long slope to Shipley Bridge. I could go on; there is plenty of time left. But I have achieved what I wanted, so I make my way down, crossing the Bala Brook near its confluence with Middle Brook, and then climb up the hill on the other side in order to rejoin the waterworks access road. Back in the Avon Valley, groups of people sit in the shade or bask in the sun. I tramp past them back to the car and for once my legs are not aching, nor are my feet sore. I have not walked very far but, by ascending the slope above the Avon Valley to the Whitebarrows, I have climbed a stepladder and peered over the top to contemplate the emptiness that lies beyond. That's all I needed to do. I head for home.

❋❋❋❋❋

14

A WALK ON THE WILD SIDE

There is a place on Dartmoor that never fails to instil in me a sense of being out in the wilderness, far removed from the hectic pace and materialism of the modern world. When it rains there, it is indescribably bleak and forbidding; when the sun shines, its solitude and wild beauty are quite breathtaking.

That place is Okement Hill. It stands more than 1,850 feet above sea-level at the northern end of a long ridge which juts out from the central morasses around Cranmere Pool. It would be typical of the rounded, grassy ridges on the northern moor were it not for the distinctive military observation post (OP15), which lies beside the military loop road at its furthest point from Okehampton. Okement Hill is an ideal point for parking and starting a walk around the central wastes of the northern moor, for even at the peak of the summer holidays, there are never many cars parked there. The only time when it can get busy is when the peace is broken by a dozen or so army lorries grinding up the road and stopping by the observation post in order to send their occupants off into the moor on a training exercise.

Okement Hill is visible from a long way off in certain directions. From places like West Mill Tor, it appears on the southern horizon and, with the observation post, together with a few army lorries parked in the immediate area, it can deceive the eye by taking on the appearance of a tor crowned by rectangular rock-stumps. On a bright day, from the slopes of Cut Hill and Black Hill to the south, it can often be identified by a tell-tale glint of sunlight from the windscreen of a car parked on its far-off summit.

One Easter, my family and I chose Okement Hill as our starting point for a walk around some of the wilder peaks of the northern moor. We left the car by the observation post and followed the rough army track south-eastwards. This track swings round into the valley of the River Taw and crosses the young river at a ford, before turning again on to the slopes above. It then joins another track which runs from Hangingstone Hill to Oke Tor. At this junction we headed south and soon found ourselves ascending the heights of Hangingstone itself. We came first to

Above: Hangingstone Hill military observation hut and flagpole.
Below: The hanging stone on Hangingstone Hill.

117

the little observation hut that sits on top of the hill and which gives the hill its distinctive profile, resembling a giant whale with a tiny pimple on its back. The hut, itself, is ugly, but it does provide some shelter from the strong wind which often can be experienced here. A couple of hundred yards down the western slope, we came across the little rock-pile with the one-time logan, or rocking stone, which gives the hill its name. Over on the eastern side, we found the steeper slopes which drop down into the deep seclusion of Watern Combe, where the Walla Brook begins its journey to the North Teign River. To the south, we could see the irregular peaty hummocks of Whitehorse Hill, half a mile away. The ridge which takes in Hangingstone and Whitehorse Hill is the second highest on the moor, being only some 60 feet lower than High Willhays and Yes Tor.

If the weather is suitable, it is worth lingering a while on the top of Hangingstone. It is one of those places which make walking on Dartmoor so special. To stand here and take in the intense solitude and vastness all around is a truly moving, spiritual experience. The mundane, commonplace worries of everyday life are banished from the mind in an instant. They are swept away by an all-pervading feeling of awe at the images of grand scale and huge distance which assault the visual senses from every direction. This sensation can only be experienced properly from the summit of the hill. As soon as one descends, even a little way, the magic spell is broken; the peak of visual experience is left behind on the hilltop.

From Hangingstone, we had an incomparable appreciation of that special ruggedness of northern Dartmoor. Ahead of us, we could see the giants of the moor; Cosdon, Belstone, Steeperton, West Mill Tor,

Wild Tor.

Yes Tor, High Willhays, Great Kneeset and Great Links. Behind us were Cut Hill and Fur Tor, while below, nearer to hand, was the great central morass, the life-source of the rivers that carve their way down through the granite to the distant Devonshire lowlands.

Such were our impressions of Hangingstone Hill that day. Rather reluctantly, we eventually moved on northwards, following the track towards our next destination, Wild Tor: the path drops down the slopes of Hangingstone and then levels out on to a plateau leading to the tor's rock-stacks, which appear prominently ahead. When we had reached the tor, we decided to descend westwards to the Steeperton Brook, unprepared for the feeling that was to come from being in this secretive, secluded valley. Hemmed in on either side by shoulders of higher ground, and with its lower end almost blocked by the great bulk of Steeperton Tor, it gave a feeling of being in a sheltered haven, a temporary respite from the blasts of westerly wind sweeping the hilltops above. It is not on any frequently-used paths or marked routes and, although the tell-tale signs of the old tin miners persist, it has about it the aura of a place where no-one ever comes or goes.

The seclusion of the valley of Steeperton Brook, with Steeperton Tor (centre) and Cosdon Hill (right) visible through the mist.

Valleys like this have their own special attraction but, after being confronted by the thrusting presence of Steeperton Tor, our next goal was already determined. It is a fairly easy climb up to the top from the upper valley of Steeperton Brook, but very much harder from any other direction. Many of Dartmoor's higher hills range in height from 1,700 to 1,900 feet above sea-level and Steeperton Tor, at 1,745 feet, fits comfortably into this category. There is the rather inevitable (for northern Dartmoor) observation hut at the north end of the summit, regrettably perched on

Steeperton Tor from the western side of Taw Valley.

top of the highest point like many of its brethren on other tors. Nevertheless, the view northwards from here is quite stunning. The River Taw and the Steeperton Brook, having squeezed around the shoulders of the tor, join forces at the foot of its northern slope, but their combined downward rush is then drastically slowed as the hills part to form the great green plain of Taw Marsh. This is like a grander version of Fox Tor Mire, its sides being bounded by some of the most spectacular heights of the moor. On the western side, the great ridge of Belstone sweeps aloft, while opposite it the slopes rise ever onwards to culminate in the massive hunched dome of Cosdon. The flatness of Taw Marsh is emphasised by the meandering course followed by the river as it snakes its way through. It is as though it were searching desperately for a way out of this enclosed amphitheatre, unwilling to accept the sudden brake imposed on its downward momentum. At the far end of Taw Marsh the hills, having relented briefly in their encroachment on the Taw Valley, crowd back in again to funnel the river through another narrow valley. Beyond there, it drops down through Belstone Cleave and off the moor to take a more sedate and dignified journey across North Devon to the sea.

Wrenching ourselves from this elevated perch, we followed the path down south-westwards to the site of Knack (or Knock) Mine. This former tin mine lies by the side of the River Taw, just upstream of Steeperton Gorge, and from it a track leads diagonally up the contours and out of the valley. As we reached the top of this track, a lone walker

Above: The view from Steeperton Tor looking across Taw Marsh towards the Belstone Tors.
Below: Steeperton Gorge.

caught us up from the south: he greeted us without stopping, explaining that he had left Ivybridge at 7 o'clock that morning and was on his way

121

to Belstone, where he intended to stop for the night. Our envy at the 24-mile epic walk which he had achieved was tempered by the thought that he would have had little, if any, chance to pause for a while and contemplate the scenery.

Moving on, we soon joined the military road and followed it south so as to return to our starting point on the top of Okement Hill, where we gratefully heaved off our boots. It was therapeutic to feel cold air playing around our bare feet after their release from many hours' confinement in boots. But, having flung off boots, socks and coats, it was not long before the cold started to penetrate and so we climbed into the car and departed. We thought back to our arrival many hours before and how the damp chill had struck us as we emerged from the warm car. It had emphasised for us the abiding impression of Okement Hill; the vastness of mile upon mile of long grass, stretching away to a distant backcloth of rugged tors to the north and round green hills to the south. Nearer to hand, young streams and peat hags are the only features which intrude upon this remorseless emptiness. The visitor to this lonely plateau will contemplate all this with an involuntary shiver, induced only in part by the chilly gusts of wind which play across it.

✳✳✳✳✳

15

GREAT KNEESET

Like some over-zealous, topographical train-spotter, I like to record all my Dartmoor walks by marking them in pencil on old copies of the two O.S. 1:50,000 scale maps which cover the moor. I can then see at a glance which parts I have not visited very frequently or, indeed, at all. After several excursions to Cranmere Pool, Fur Tor, Hare Tor, Tavy Cleave and Bleak House, it became apparent from the pencilled routes that it was high time that I went to the area bounded by all these locations: the prominent features in this desolate patch of the moor are Amicombe Hill and Great Kneeset.

The theme of my chosen outward route was one of following a diminishing river valley upstream from a deep gouge through towering rock-cliffs to the flat, anonymous grassy uplands of the inner moor. My eldest son and I made this journey one warm July day after our usual dawn start from home. We parked at Lane Head and followed the Wheal Friendship Leat round into Tavy Cleave. In the height of this particularly dry summer, the flow in the Tavy was very low and the stark, boulder-strewn hillsides were softened by a carpet of green bracken. This was a quite different impression from what we had experienced in our previous visit to Tavy Cleave. On that occasion, the late October frosts had already stripped the hills of bright green and overpainted them in autumnal brown, while the valley echoed with the incessant burble of tumbling water. But, on this day, we had to don hats to protect ourselves from the merciless, blinding heat of the sun, and every waft of breeze up that sheltered canyon was welcomed with relief. Just for once, we could not wait to get out of this normally delightful spot.

On reaching Rattlebrook Foot we were, at last, exposed to some moving air, only for my son, whose ever-growing feet were now big enough for him to wear my wife's walking boots for the first time, to start complaining of a blistered heel. Impatiently, I told him what I thought of his endurance after only one and a half miles of a seven or eight mile walk. In response he promptly reminded me in no uncertain terms that it had been my idea that he should borrow the boots in the first place, and

The narrow valley of the Tavy above Rattlebrook Foot.

that, if he had had his way, he would have worn his old, but comfortable, trainers. At that point I realised that his powers of argument were growing as rapidly as his feet, so I applied antiseptic cream, together with some layers of sticking plaster, and, with peace restored, we carried on up the valley of the Tavy.

Our path alongside the river now swung south-eastwards, face first into the sun. The valley was still narrow, but becoming shallower all the while. Above us, to the left, were the many hut circles of Watern Oke, half-buried in bracken. The going on the hillside path was slow and rough, with much boulder-hopping, but as the path turned to the east so the narrow neck of the valley widened out again. To our right, the Western Redlake joined the Tavy from the south, and it was now, at last, that we were able to leave the rocky, uneven path behind and to emerge, gratefully, on to the short, dry turf at the southern tip of Amicombe Hill.

The character of the Tavy Valley had now changed markedly. From a steep, rocky cleft, our surroundings were suddenly transformed into the gentle contours of a young river valley as we made our way upstream. In fact, as it descends from its source, the Tavy is augmented by a number of other streams. These include Amicombe Brook, Black Ridge Brook, Cut Combe Water, Fur Tor Brook and Eastern Redlake. But all the while it remains a gently flowing upland stream and it is not until it is joined by the Western Redlake that the character of the Tavy landscape changes from grassy slopes to rocky defile. Then it is almost as if the waters of the Western Redlake give the Tavy that final increment of energy necessary for it to begin cutting down into the underlying rock.

As the Tavy Valley declined in scale, so our view over the high moor became ever more panoramic. Dominating this wider prospect to the east was the huge profile of Fur Tor, which now hove gracefully into view like some grand ocean-going liner. In front of it, like a green bow-wave, was the rounded hill known as Pinswell, while in the distance the top of Little Kneeset formed the skyline.

We eventually parted company with the River Tavy at Sandy Ford, where we joined the Amicombe Brook and carried on upstream on its true right bank to the point where it swung round to come at us from the north. As it did so, we found ourselves in a broader valley, an upland bowl surrounded by green hills. The rim of the bowl was formed by Little Kneeset, Black Hill, Black Ridge and Great Kneeset, our destination for that day. Behind us now, across a sea of green flecked by white cotton grass, Fur Tor was a massive black hulk, with its central rock-stump silhouetted like a ship's funnel against the southern sky. To our left, we could see along the eastern slope of Amicombe Hill, the anonymous giant of the northern moor. Looking directly up to the head of the valley, the rim of the bowl was punctured by Broad Amicombe

Sandy Ford on the Tavy, with Fur Tor beyond.

Hole: through this natural aperture we could see Black Tor perched on the slopes of High Willhays, and Yes Tor away to the north. Nearer to hand, the uniformity of the wet green levels was punctuated every so often by small humps of peat overgrown with whortleberry. Nowhere was any sign of human life to be seen.

Great Kneeset was now clearly visible about a mile away, the intervening ground rising and then levelling out before the final slope to the summit rocks. But it was now that we (that is, I) made the mistake of deciding to follow a straight-line course over what looked like easy ground. Only when it was too late to turn round did we realise that we had strayed on to that especially awkward type of surface which Dartmoor has a habit of springing on to the unwary. Deep grass overlay the remains of old peat workings, and we had no choice other than to drag our legs through it, ankle muscles straining with the unevenness under our feet. It was also quite boggy in places and, had the summer not been dry, we would have had to flounder back to the Amicombe Brook to find a better route. We had realised too late that what we should have done, at an earlier stage, was to have gone eastwards to Black Ridge, along the peat pass and then westwards to Great Kneeset.

After the first half-mile or so, as the ground began to rise, we came across two fresh, circular holes about three or four feet across and three feet deep. Now why, we wondered, should anyone come all the way out here with a spade and dig these holes? And why were there no heaps of spoil around the holes? It took my brain, addled as it was by exhaustion and strong sunlight, a minute or two to realise that the spoil was spread far and wide because the holes had not been dug at all. We were, of course, in the Okehampton Firing Range, and the holes had been caused by exploding mortars!

The summit rocks of Great Kneeset.

On we pressed up the slope of Great Kneeset before finally flinging ourselves down to rest, to have lunch and to carry out a blister inspection. When the agonies of fatigue, hunger, thirst and soreness had receded we were able to relax and take in the extraordinary solitude of our surroundings. The view north was dominated by Lints Tor and the valley of the West Okement, where the green sprawl of Black-a-tor Copse crept tentatively up the eastern slope. To the north-east was the curve of Okement Hill, crowned by the little observation post, while round to the north-west, Stenga Tor and Kitty Tor looked small and lost on the whale-back of Amicombe Hill. Round still further, Amicombe Hill appeared to have grown a new, larger rock-pile: it took a moment to realise that this was, in fact, Great Links Tor peeping over from beyond the skyline. Immediately north of us, the ground fell steeply away to where the West Okement River, hidden from our view, wound tortuously along the foot of the slope.

After an hour or so we threw our rucksacks back on and set off on the return journey. Heading west, we passed above the steep drop down to the West Okement, where the river almost turns back on itself, and walked down into the curious little gully that runs over the watershed between the Amicombe Brook and a feeder stream of the West Okement, to form Broad Amicombe Hole. On we went up the steep, but firm slopes of Amicombe Hill, before breasting the top of the ridge and

Above: The cloud shadows give definition to the valley of the West Okement in this view from Great Kneeset across to Amicombe Hill.

Below: The view southwards through Broad Amicombe Hole.

heading on down into the valley of the Rattlebrook. Soon we were passing through the extensive, long-abandoned tin workings that lie between

Green Tor Water and the stream known as The Scad. A third stream flows down through these tin workings and they all meet just above the Rattlebrook before flowing into it.

As we neared the bottom of the hill we disturbed a fox, the first we had ever seen on the moor even though we had come across innumerable foxes' earths over the years. It had a peculiarly bright orange, shaggy coat, which I am told is a distinctive feature of the Dartmoor fox. The speed at which it disappeared contrasted greatly with the carefree tameness of a suburban fox that stood on the pavement and watched me drive past on my way to work a few weeks afterwards.

Not wanting to go back through the fierce heat in the shelter of Tavy Cleave, we opted to stay in the breeze and to take the rough track that leads diagonally upwards across the face of Hare Tor. Fatigue was now setting in, and it seemed like a lifetime before we reached Ger Tor and finally dropped down to our car at Lane Head. Nevertheless, we did at least have the satisfaction of knowing that we had completed a hard walk to yet another remote spot in the fastness of the moor, one to where there is no really easy route because it is well off any beaten tracks such as there are on the northern moor.

We headed home and later that night, just before falling asleep, I remembered that I had not pencilled in the route on my map. The next day, this omission was rectified to record the fact that my meagre knowledge of the moor had taken yet another step forward. Far more important than a mere increase in the number of walks marked on my map, was the deep feeling of fulfilment that came from having left the material world behind for a day in order to cleanse the soul in the challenging beauty of Dartmoor.

16

SOGGY, BOGGY AND FOGGY

It was a Friday, the day before the start of the October half-term. My family and I had booked a week away on Dartmoor at one of our favourite holiday houses in Shaugh Prior. Already walking on air, I cleared my desk at work and headed home to pack, in the knowledge that on the following day we would be going out on to the north-eastern part of the moor to explore that tucked-away section between Throwleigh and Gidleigh Commons. It is an area that is visited less than others by walkers and tourists, and all the better for it: we, ourselves, had not been there very often. A glance at the map shows that it is also an area with a lot of marshy ground but, at the same time, with a number of useful, long-established tracks leading out into its heart.

The next day we made our usual early arrival on the moor. The hills were just visible in translucent profile through the thin mist enveloping the mid-Devon countryside that autumn morning. Branching off the road between South Zeal and Throwleigh, we drove up the narrow road which skirts the moor en route to Moortown. To our left, beyond the enclosure wall, the ground fell steeply away towards Throwleigh. On the other side, our view over the moor was blocked by the steep shoulder of Throwleigh Common, dressed in its autumnal garb of dying bracken.

Parking by the wall where the verge was wide enough, we shackled ourselves into backpacks, coats and boots. It was a pleasant thought that today's visit was no brief, fleeting affair, but the start of a full week's holiday. We took the path marked on the map which runs from near the disused quarry, directly up the slopes of the common and on to its firm summit. Soon we were dropping into the valley of the Blackaton Brook, following a path known as the Gallaven Track. Crossing the brook at a ford, our path now became sunken and we realised that by using this moorland track we were following in the footsteps of many long-departed moormen and peat-cutters. For those people the firm formation of the track had eased, in a small, but welcome way, the burden of making a modest living out of the remote heights that lay ahead of us. Now, as it took us round the hill, following the brook upstream ever more steeply, it was making easier our walk of leisure into the heart of the moor.

Soon we were crossing the brook again at another ford, only in this instance very rough and rocky. Beyond, the ground levelled out and we found ourselves gazing westwards over the dark, menacing, wetland grass of Raybarrow Pool. Often on the moor we will try to cross level ground which, from its appearance, is clearly wet in places; but one glance at the sinister levels that now lay before us made it all too plain that such tactics would be foolhardy in the extreme. At the edge of Raybarrow Pool, we inspected the two boundstones that mark the boundary of the parishes of South Tawton and Throwleigh. Then, on we went along the Gallaven Track as it turned southwards round the western flank of Kennon Hill. The mist was still with us, but every so often we caught a glimpse, as if through a net curtain, of the enormous domed outline of Cosdon Hill, a mile away to the north-west.

We were walking now along the secluded valley between Kennon Hill and the great ridge which takes in Cosdon, Little Hound Tor and Hound Tor. The mist began to close in upon us as we neared the boundary stone on the extreme south-eastern corner of the South Tawton parish boundary. Next we sought to go over the marshy ground to the west of this boundary stone and find White Moor Circle. Unlike Raybarrow, the ground was squelchy, but easily crossed. The mist swirled around us, creating a feeling of foreboding and mystery about what lay ahead. Suddenly we stopped as a tall figure wearing a pointed cowl loomed up menacingly on the slope ahead of us. Was this some spectral monk seeking to lure us to some awful fate? Would he wreak some terrible retribution upon us for invading the sanctity of his lonely domain? The figure remained unmoved, but its ghostly appearance faded from our imagination as we continued and quickly discovered that it was just the austere, but reassuring, outline of White Moor Stone.

With relief we looked around and could now see, through the fog, the outlines of the stones forming the White Moor Circle. Beyond them the ground disappeared upwards into the white nothingness shrouding Little Hound Tor. In the stillness and silence we imagined the presence of countless ghosts of all those who had ever passed by this place, principally ancient man, who had erected the stone circle and the standing stone for some purpose as yet undiscovered, and also, thousands of years later, those people who, subsequent to earlier perambulations, chose the sentinel-like monolith as one of the Forest boundary markers. In the enveloping fog, we sensed the infinite mystery of this isolated spot, which had been important to generations of man stretching far back into the depths of time.

From White Moor Stone, we set off to the south-west, making for Hound Tor. Reaching the top of the first slope, we looked around fruitlessly in the mist for the rocks of the tor – before glancing at the map and realising that Hound Tor was actually at the top of the next rise; we

Above: White Moor Stone. The inscriptions 'DC' (Duchy of Cornwall) and 'TP' (Throwleigh Parish) can be seen on the face of the stone.

Below: White Moor Circle, with White Moor Stone beyond, to the left.

had only reached its northern flank. Accurate map reading is as important as using the compass in such conditions.

As we gained the summit of Hound Tor a window in the mist floated past and, through it, we glimpsed Steeperton Tor and the strange ramp-like profile of Metheral Hill. We wanted now to get to Gallaven Ford, which lay to the south-east. Gallaven Ford is called Gartaven Ford by the Ordnance Survey even though it crosses the Gallaven Brook, whose name appears as such on the map. This is just one of the eccentricities perpetrated on the map of Dartmoor by the O.S. In his book entitled *High Dartmoor*, Eric Hemery demonstrates time and again how the Ordnance Survey have unintentionally corrupted old names and misplaced others. It would be nice to think that one day these will be corrected for as time passes it will become harder to change the status quo of the place-names shown on the map.

Hound Tor and the Steeperton Brook, as seen from Steeperton Tor.

A straight course meant a direct crossing of Gallaven Mire and so we chose, instead, to head south and then to skirt the southern edge of the mire in order to reach the ford. As we descended, the mist finally began to clear and soon a milky sun showed itself through the higher cloud before breaking through to give a belatedly bright morning. We located the Sandy Road, another old track which runs from Wild Tor Well, over Headon (a hill at grid reference SX631 880, but not named on the map) and Gallaven Ford. It then passes to the north of Rival Tor, skirts Whitemoor Marsh and leaves the moor at Buttern. After crossing Gallaven Ford, we left this track to drop down into the valley of Gallaven Brook and then up on to Rival Tor.

The view from Rival Tor was quite breathtaking. It is a little promontory of high ground projecting into the great sepia-brown plain of the North Teign and the Walla Brook. Between us and the far-off heights of the southern moor, the coniferous blanket of Fernworthy Forest draped itself over the hills, seemingly resisting their contorted efforts to shake off this gloomy shroud. The wall of the Teignhead Newtake crossed the North Teign above the steep side of Manga Hole and climbed at a dizzy angle out of the valley, while the stark, anvil-like profile of Watern Tor rock-stack stood out prominently on the south-western skyline, the apparent hole visible, like the eye of a distant needle.

With time moving on, we dragged ourselves away from this spectacular panorama and walked on along the foot of the eastern slope of Kennon Hill, keeping clear of Whitemoor Marsh. This wet area feeds the Forder Brook and, once its little valley had started to appear, we followed the left bank downstream. When we were well down the valley, we cut across to the miniature Shilstone Tor (not to be confused with Shelstone Tor on the slope of Corn Ridge, above the West Okement) and made our way along the slope to our car.

The last time that my wife and I had been on this part of the moor was when returning from our first visit to Cranmere Pool, back in 1982. On that occasion we were walking in the extreme heat of high summer, but today we had been through thick mist. Although this had restricted our visual impressions of the moor, it had strengthened the sensation of being in a wild, untamed landscape. This is a place that has rejected the advances made to it by civilisation: it remains aloof and aloft among the hills.

17

WHITEHORSE HILL

I have just driven the 175 miles or so from home and arrived at Batworthy a few minutes past 7.30 on a November morning to set off on a walk to Whitehorse Hill and back. There is an icy tang to the air and the grass is white with frost, but one other car is here already. It transpires that it belongs to a local resident, who suddenly appears over the hill with his three dogs, their rapid, excited breath crystalline in the cold air. We greet one another and then I'm off, alone, on to Shovel Down. Reaching the top of the ridge above the Longstone, the gloomy coniferous cohorts of Fernworthy Forest appear ahead, reminding me that I could have shortened my walk by setting out from the innermost car park of the forest. But, having undergone the depressing trek of $1^1/4$ miles through the deep shadow of the pine trees once before, I had resolved never to do so again. In any event, as far as I am concerned Fernworthy Forest is completely alien to Dartmoor.

Crossing the brilliant, sunlit, open heights of Shovel Down, the normally soft ground is frozen hard and proving wonderful to walk over. All too soon, though, I am moving from the sparkling vigour of the open down into the morbid, Siberian shadow of Fernworthy Forest, and am obliged to follow its northern flank down into the valley of the North Teign; on the opposite slope the stone ruins of Manga Farm sprout out of the dead bracken. Further round, the remains of Teignhead Farm and its enclosures are thrown into relief by long, early morning, shadows, and I must now make my way there by crossing the river at the Teignhead clapper bridge and then following the track around to the farm entrance. The walls of the house may now only be a few feet above the ground, having been demolished in 1971, but the ruins are pregnant with the traces of the former occupants. Furthermore, the little enclosed 'home paddocks', the stone trough and the slotted gateposts all point to the farm's history as a serious going concern from the early 1800s until the 1930s. In the distance the wall of the Teignhead Newtake sweeps down from Sittaford Tor into the valley of the North Teign and out of sight towards the heights of Quinter's Man.

My route now takes me uphill, through the northernmost 'home paddock'

Teignhead clapper bridge.

The ruins of Teignhead Farm.

137

Slotted gatepost at Teignhead Farm.

and alongside a stream that tumbles down the slope from a rocky lip high above the enclosures of the farm. According to the O.S. map, this stream is called Manga Brook but, in *High Dartmoor,* Eric Hemery states that, historically, moormen have known it as the Great Mire Stream, which is certainly appropriate. After quite a stiff climb alongside the stream, the ground levels out and one can see into the bowl of the Great Mire itself; it is like a perched, dry lake, and Hemery believed that it may, indeed, once have been filled with water until the tinners drained it in their search for the mineral. On the far side, the slope of the huge Whitehorse-Hangingstone ridge soars aloft.

Going across the Great Mire, I keep to the left of the obvious wetter areas and appreciate even then that the frozen ground forgives several steps which would normally have resulted in a wet foot. Reaching the far side, I glance back and notice that, whilst the tops of the trees in Fernworthy can still be seen, Teignhead Farm is hidden below the lip of the mire; I don't look for long because the sun is shining directly and ferociously into my eyes. Instead, I start the long climb up the slope, heading for the range notice board high above me, beyond the newtake wall. My steps become shorter and slower, and my heartbeat races in my ears. Gasping, I come thankfully to the wall and stop for a first swig of my cold orange juice.

From the range notice board a distinct path heads off to the north-west and I soon find the head of Watern Combe coming into view as the ground levels out. Down in this sombre combe, bounded by Hangingstone Hill to the west and Watern Tor to the east, the rainwater is collected and runs away as the Walla Brook; eventually it joins the North Teign at Teign-e-ver, at the foot of Scorhill Down. Meanwhile, I now have to look out for the Sand Path, a raised causeway about 300 yards long over the flat fen, and then, after finding it, swing round into Whitehorse Hill peat pass from its northern end.

Whitehorse Hill peat pass.

On reaching the eastern end of the peat pass, one of many dug out at around the end of the 19th century by Frank Phillpotts of Okehampton (but, in this instance, deepened by the military authorities during the 1960s), I am greeted by one of the original marker stones with a commemorative plaque. Now, at last, I really am on Whitehorse Hill and, spurred on by more than a little tinge of excitement, I walk through the peat pass to its western end, by the Whitehorse cairn. Here, the original marker stone went missing many years ago, as did the one at the upper end of the peat pass on the western slope of the hill, but, in 1988, replicas were erected, entirely appropriately, by the Dartmoor National Park Authority. It is the view, though, that is now attracting my attention. Half a mile to the north is the summit of Hangingstone Hill with its observation hut, while behind me, to the east, lies my outward route from Fernworthy; beyond it the Devonshire lowlands disappear away into the frosted mist on the skyline. Most important of all so far as I am concerned, however, is the view to the west, for on my way out from Batworthy this extended only to the slopes of the enormous whale-back, whose summit I have finally reached. Now, at last, I can see beyond it to the desolate central plateau of the northern moor, where Black Hill, Cut Hill and Fur Tor gaze fixedly over their lonely domain. I feel, yet again, that tremendous surge of excitement that comes from being in this, the remotest part of the whole moor. It is the pinnacle of all the sensations that Dartmoor can offer.

A stiff breeze drives the cold into me and so I look to my next destination, Quinter's Man, which is a mile away to the south. I follow a very firm track and this leads me close to Moute's Inn, one of several ruined peat-cutters' shelters hereabouts. On the western side of the hilltop

The ruins of Moute's Inn, a peat-cutter's shelter on Whitehorse Hill.

the abandoned peat workings show clearly the depth to which the peat was removed. As I walk along the top of the ridge, the complexity of the topography is also apparent. Initially, the East Dart flows at the foot of the western slope, but then a spur of higher ground, Kit Hill, breaks away from Whitehorse Hill to form an intermediate combe in which the North Teign River is born.

I soon reach Quinter's Man, where I sit inside the shelter of the walled

Above: Quinter's Man cairn, which affords some shelter on this lonely hilltop.

Below: Military paraphernalia comprising two huts, flagpole and range boundary pole spoil the view at Quinter's Man.

cairn. The immediate view is rather spoilt by the two army observation huts and the flagpole, but even these cannot detract from the prospect over the valley of the North Teign and the high empty hills beyond. It is the first time that I have ever been to Quinter's Man and it impresses me deeply. I walk over to its eastern flank and gaze down into the steep-sided valley of the Varracombe Brook, contemplating its intense solitude.

According to Eric Hemery in *High Dartmoor*, the names Little Varracombe and Great Varracombe have been entirely misplaced by the Ordnance Survey. He believed that the former is the small hill to the east of Quinter's Man, between it and the North Teign, and that Great Varracombe was actually Quinter's Man. This gets very confusing, especially as Quinter's Man is then referred to on the O.S. map as Quintin's Man. It is as though there was some Home Counties tendency at work in the O.S. map-name department seeking to make this bleak hilltop sound more welcoming – by varying its name so as to be reminiscent of some kindly uncle in an Enid Blyton adventure story!

I look at the map and assess the options for my return journey, unsure of which route offers the most. Eventually, I decide to bring my indecisiveness to an end and set off down into the combe of Teign Head (that is Teign Head proper, not the ruined farm 2 miles downstream), heading for the large boulder that stands with other rocks on the west side of the young stream. To my surprise, I cross the marshy valley floor without difficulty and then I follow the river downstream, as it curves erratically around the foot of Quinter's Man. Soon I approach the point where the wall of the Teignhead Newtake crosses the river, and it is here that I decide to throw down my coat on to a sheltered mound of heather and have lunch. It is still only a quarter past mid-day, but I have been walking for 4½ hours – and I am hungry!

Moving on feeling nourished once more, I enter the little steep-sided cut that is upstream of the confluence with the Varracombe Brook and find that the south bank, having been in shadow all morning, is still white with frost. I am not here for long, though, before the trees on the western edge of the Teignhead Farm plantation appear over the hilltop and beckon me in their direction. There is also a surprise in store; as I reach the plantation so my eye is caught by a movement on the opposite slope below Fernworthy Forest. The horses of the local hunt are moving slowly along it. Then they stop, the riders looking in my direction. A sound from behind causes me to turn and I can now see a forest of pointed tails moving methodically through the stumps and long grass of the felled plantation. The hounds were there all the time and I had completely failed to spot them. Suddenly one gives an excited yelp by a pile of branches around a tree stump. Needing no second bidding, his colleagues burst into a yowling cacophany and bound over to assist. A huntsman pulls away some of the branches as the hordes scramble to get at the scent. There is clearly a strong smell of fresh fox in the air, but its source must be in safety, underground. If the fox is foolish enough to come out, it will not live for more than a few seconds. Wisely, it stays put and the hounds are eventually called off. Subsequently, a four-wheeled off-road vehicle goes across the Teignhead clapper and on into the farm, then stops as men with spades and a gun emerge from it. As I move on so they begin to dig, but no shots are heard and I feel gladdened that this sensible fox has, seemingly, survived the day.

I go up onto the hillside and follow the walled track that leads through the ruins of Manga Farm. This spot is as intriguing as Teignhead Farm, albeit that the ruins are on a much smaller scale. Manga Farm house was not occupied for very long and apparently ended up as a storage barn. Its location on this hillside must have made it a lovely place to live in summer and, even now, it is more cheerful than Teignhead, whose surrounding trees give its ruins a distinct air of gloom.

The ruins of Manga Farm.

After clambering down the hillside, I cross the river above Manga Hole. Here the North Teign abandons its slack meanders and rushes down a steep rocky slope, only to resume its gentle wandering once more at the foot. The deep afternoon shadow cannot hide the great beauty of this secluded cleft in the hills, but, eventually, I have to leave what is the last milestone of my day's walk behind and concentrate on getting back to Batworthy. As I cross Shovel Down every shadowed dip and hollow is yet white with frost, and will remain so, for the sun is now

The secluded beauty of Manga Hole.

well on its way down. Far away on the other side of the North Teign basin the voices of the huntsmen and the cries of the hounds carry clearly on the still, cold air of late afternoon.

As I arrive back at the car I reflect on what an incredible day it has been. The brilliant sunlight, the hard, frozen ground underfoot and the lofty heights of Whitehorse Hill have etched in me another indelible Dartmoor memory. I had been in two minds whether to come, having previously experienced the biting cold of the moorland winter. But my fears had been groundless; instead, it has been one of the most memorable days that I have ever spent on the moor.

✳✳✳✳✳

18

DARTMOOR NORTH AND SOUTH

On many occasions in this book I use the terms 'northern Dartmoor' and 'the southern moor' as though they were two separate entities. And that's exactly what they are, at least to anyone like me who goes on to the moor for the specific purpose of walking over its remotest parts.

Geologically, of course, Dartmoor is a single feature. But geographically, roads, agriculture and human habitation have encroached on to part of its surface, taking away some of the original open moorland. Four roads, for example, cross the moor scissors-like and meet at Two Bridges, creating a swathe of civilisation which bisects it. Between the 'handles' and 'blades' of the scissors, there are, I grant, significant areas of moorland. These include the King's Tor and Foggintor Quarry area, Bellever and Laughter Tor, Yar Tor and Corndon Tor, Hameldown, and Hay Tor and Hound Tor. But agriculture has crept into these areas along the river valleys of the Walkham, the East and West Dart, and the East and West Webburn. Settlements, such as Widecombe, Hexworthy and Buckland have sprung up. The development of Princetown, itself, with its prison and the needs of its population, has led to the enclosure of substantial areas of adjacent land for agriculture. Moreover, much of the eastern side of Dartmoor, while very picturesque, has been enclosed for farming owing to its more sheltered position and lower, less exposed landscape.

Consequently, looking at the whole area of the Dartmoor National Park, the two remaining areas of true wilderness are to be found in its north-western and south-western quadrants. Between them is a central basin, comprising several river valleys. The combined size of the wilderness areas is relatively small; whilst the total area of the National Park is 368 square miles, I estimate that the northern wilderness occupies about 77 square miles and the southern wilderness about 49 square miles: together, they occupy only about a third of the National Park. These statistics alone serve to illustrate just how important it is to protect the wilderness areas that remain and to ensure that no further encroachment into them is allowed.

I would not, however, contend that the areas of non-wilderness are lacking in natural beauty. Quite the contrary – the general landscape is one where a patchwork quilt of small fields is spread out over domed foothills, and many of the river valleys are thickly wooded. I well remember driving from Buckland-in-the-Moor to Newbridge one autumn morning, having taken a wrong turning. All around me the woodland floor was carpeted in brown bracken and, below, the River Dart tumbled its way around a mass of grey boulders. Enhanced by the effects of light and shadow created by the early morning sun, the scene was one of quite stunning beauty. It was also a fitting aperitif for the long walk that I was about to undertake over the southern moor. Apart from the lower levels, there are areas of high moor between and next to the roads, such as Hay Tor, Honeybag Tor, King's Tor and Bellever. These hills are too high and exposed to have fallen to agriculture in the manner of the lowlands at their foot and, instead, form a magnificent backdrop to the lush green valleys around them, albeit without the special wilderness characteristics.

Returning to the northern and southern wildernesses, let's examine them more closely and see if we can identify similarities and differences in their character. They are both, of course, at a relatively high altitude and subject to a prevailing south-westerly airstream. With that comes high annual rainfall – 60 inches per year on average, and 80 inches per year at Princetown. A number of important rivers are, therefore, born in the middle of each wilderness. The East and West Okement, East and West Dart, Tavy, Walkham, Taw, Teign and Lyd begin life in the high northern morasses. At the centre of the southern wastes are the sources of the Plym, Yealm, Erme and Avon. The rivers of the northern moor drain off in all directions, whilst those of the south flow predominantly southwards. The valley system of the northern area is, therefore, larger and more intricate than that of the south.

The greatest distinction between the two areas, apart from size, is, of course, the use by the army of large parts of the northern wilderness for live firing. The three ranges, Okehampton, Merrivale and Willsworthy, occupy 52 out of the 77 square miles that make up the northern area. The largest range, Okehampton, is open to the public for 253 days each year, the Merrivale range is open for 192 days and the smallest range, Willsworthy, is open for 124 days. While some people object to the restrictions to access which stem from live firing, it does, as I have stated previously, serve to keep walkers off this part of the moor for certain periods and to deter casual visitors.

Features such as hut circles, stone circles, stone rows, kistvaens, tinners' huts and old tin workings are to be found in the north and in the south. But the peat passes, with the exception of Black Lane on the southern moor (which is, in any case, largely natural rather than man-made), are found only in the north. This could be because Frank

Don't say that you weren't warned! Okehampton Firing Range warning notice on Green Tor above Bleak House.

Phillpotts, who instigated the digging out of the more recent peat passes, was a resident of Okehampton and probably not unduly concerned with problems presented to a horse rider trying to cross the distant southern moor. It could also be argued that there was a greater abundance of tracks across the smaller southern wilderness. This, along with the more favourable layout of the river valleys and more passable terrain, meant that, by and large, peat passes were unnecessary in the south. The single peat pass on the southern moor, Black Lane, is a convenient route over the watershed between the Swincombe and the Erme and serves to illustrate that the peat passes sprung up out of necessity rather than whim. Incidentally, Black Lane, and Cut Lane on the northern moor, are believed to be very much older than the other peat passes dug out on the north moor by Frank Phillpotts between 1885 and 1905.

By comparison with the northern wilderness, the southern wilderness is also distinctly lacking in tors, being generally less rugged, but with huge, gradual green slopes at its heart. By my reckoning, of the 152 named tors on the O.S. 1:25,000 walkers' map of Dartmoor, 65 of them are in the northern wilderness, but there are only 20 in the southern. In addition, there are tors which are not named on any O.S. map. These tend to be rocky stumps left over on the side of a much bigger ridge, having resisted, more stubbornly, the erosive forces that wore down their surroundings. One example is Over Tor, which sits on the approach slope to Great Mis Tor above the Walkham Valley, near

Merrivale. As far as remoteness is concerned, the furthest point on the northern moor, 4 miles from civilisation, is the area between Black Ridge and Black Hill, not far from Cranmere Pool. Similarly, in the southern wilderness, the area between Dry Lake and Green Hill is the most isolated, being around 3 miles out from the fringes of the tamed moorland.

So much for statistics. But what about walking in these wildernesses? Do they arouse different feelings in the walker who ventures out into their midst?

There is no doubt that, in bad weather, both areas can be extremely hostile and forbidding, even to the properly equipped walker who knows the moor well. With reduced visibility and a lack of many distinct landmarks, anyone without a compass, north moor or south moor regardless, is in serious trouble, particularly in winter. But, even in good conditions, I confess that I always think that little bit harder before I go into the northern wilderness. If I'm going out to its heart, my round trip will be 2 miles longer than the equivalent walk on the southern moor. I will need to plan my route carefully, especially if it is winter when daylight hours are short. Quite apart from those considerations, I will also need to check the firing programme for the three ranges on the northern moor.

To walk in the heart of the northern wilderness is the ultimate Dartmoor experience. The sense of isolation is intense; the empty landscape is all-enveloping, absorbing the lone walker on to its face. The enormous sky, the huge scale of the terrain and the sense of permanent, untouched wildness serve to emphasise the miniscule importance of anyone venturing over the moor for a few brief hours. Out here, there are fewer obvious traces of man than there are on the southern moor; and fewer comforting waymarks left by human hand. No Broad Rock, no Eylesbarrow Cairn, no posts like those near Caters Beam to show the way into and out of Black Lane; but plenty of stumbling over Tavy Head, many acres of anonymity around Walkham Head, and the immensity of Cut Hill and Black Hill is there for all to see ... if there is no mist.

This is the main contrast between the two areas of Dartmoor so far as I am concerned. Unlike the northern moor, a walk out to the centre of the southern moor leaves me with a distinct feeling that the tide of human activity once rose this far, but has now receded to the fringes of the moor, hopefully never to return. At its heart is the upland idyll of Erme Head, around which one can see the many signs of human presence past; the remains of the centuries-old tin mine at Erme Pits; the inscribed marker stones of Broad Rock and A Head; and the stone row that ends on Green Hill. Through it all runs the old Jobbers' Road (or 'Abbots' Way' as the Ordnance Survey insists on calling it), which, according to the late Eric Hemery in his book *Walking Dartmoor's Ancient Tracks* was used by wool-merchants (or jobbers) to travel from Sheepstor to Buckfastleigh. In the heart of the southern moor the feeling of isolation that it arouses is accompanied by a sensation that many long-gone generations have trodden these paths. They are now vanished into dust, but we still see their marker stones and the remains of their works. In reality, of course, the northern moor has been as much trodden by human foot as the southern. But I am thinking more about the impressions given by the landscape and the traces on it, rather than its detailed workaday history. To me, the important and special aspects of walking on Dartmoor are the sensations it brings. Any book about walking on Dartmoor which becomes a relentless catalogue of detail, misses the entire impact of the place.

As for my preference, northern or southern wilderness, I have none. They are each wonderful places to go, to clear the mind of the trivialities of everyday life. Out there, one can contemplate the primeval forces of nature which created the moor and discover the traces left by man in his hopeless attempts to live and work on it. Whenever I return home from a day's walking on the moor, I immediately start to plan my next visit. I cannot get enough of the place; I cannot wait for my next escape to Dartmoor.

BIBLIOGRAPHY

I have listed below some books and periodicals which cover various aspects of Dartmoor. The list is nowhere near to being exhaustive, but represents a useful collection of reading material for anyone wishing to follow up with more Dartmoor impressions as well as to obtain more detailed information about any subject mentioned in this book. In producing this work, I have been able to use these publications as a source of reference for which, in each instance, I acknowledge with thanks the work of the author concerned.

The Dartmoor National Park information centres at Princetown, Postbridge, Haytor, Newbridge, Okehampton, Tavistock and Ivybridge stock a good selection of books which are still in print. In addition, there are new and secondhand bookshops in many of the towns on the periphery of the moor. Alternatively, periodicals such as the *Dartmoor Magazine* (see below) advertise a good range of books available by post from various publishers.

I have included, in my selection of books, *High Dartmoor* by the late Eric Hemery, which is difficult to obtain and expensive (£65 in 1995), but is a real tour de force as a readable reference book; it is comprehensive (over 1,000 pages) and reasonably modern (published in 1983, reprinted in 1992), yet is far from being a dry and tedious catalogue of detail. The author's deep affection for the moor and its people makes a memorable impression on the reader. I obtained my copy by a chance remark in an Ashburton bookshop about how keen I was to obtain it, and could not believe my luck when the owner drew out her only sale copy from under the counter.

Here then is the list:–

A Field Guide to Boundary Markers on and around Dartmoor, by Dave Brewer. Published by Devon Books in 1986. An interesting guide to the great variety of boundary stones on the moor.

Crossing's Dartmoor Worker, by William Crossing. A collection of articles written by Crossing for the *Western Morning News* and most recently published by Peninsula Press in 1992. Available in hardback and softback.

Dartmoor Forest Farms, by Elisabeth Stanbrook. Published by Devon Books in 1994. Detailed and original research into the history of nine farms of the high moor by the editor of the *Dartmoor Magazine.*

Dartmoor's Greatest Walk, by Bill Ransom. Published by Devon Books in 1987. A good, detailed description of the route around the boundary of the Forest of Dartmoor for anyone wishing to carry out their own personal perambulation.

Dartmoor Letterboxes, by Anne Swinscow. Published by Kirkford Publications in 1984, with subsequent reprints. Describes the hobby of letter-boxing on the moor; written by the wife of the man who formed the 'Dartmoor Letterboxers' 100 Club'.

Exploring Dartmoor, by F. H. Starkey. A good introductory guide to walks on the moor. First published by the late author in 1980. (Subsequently revised and updated by Eric Thurlow, and published by Peninsula Press in 1995). Its companion volume is:–

Exploring Dartmoor Again, by F. H. Starkey. Builds on the work of its predecessor (see above). First published by the late author in 1981.

Guide to Dartmoor, by William Crossing. The classic Dartmoor work. A reprint of the 1912 edition was most recently published by Peninsula Press in 1990 and is still available in hardback and softback.

High Dartmoor, by Eric Hemery. Published by Robert Hale in 1983 and reprinted in 1992. Hard to obtain and cost £65 in 1995. Comes boxed when new. A collector's item already, quite apart from its status as one man's life-time study and experience of the moor.

The Hound of the Baskervilles, by Sir Arthur Conan Doyle. This superb work gave me my first impressions of Dartmoor, and what impressions they were! Quite apart from the story, itself, the reader's mind is impregnated with the vision of the moor as a deeply mysterious landscape overhung by an ever-present sense of menace and foreboding. I first read the book when I was aged ten and it made me long to see and explore the moor for myself. My only regret is that nearly 20 years passed before I could begin to fulfil this ambition.

The story was first published as a serial in the *Strand Magazine* in 1901 and then by George Newnes as a book in 1902.

The Redlake Tramway and China Clay Works, by E. A. Wade. Published by Twelveheads Press in 1982, but unfortunately now out of print. A compre-hensive and readable record of this remarkable enterprise.

Walking Dartmoor's Ancient Tracks, by Eric Hemery. Published by Robert Hale in 1986. A guide to 28 old routes across and within the moor. Like *High Dartmoor*, the book leaves the reader with a clear sense that here is the work of a man who was uniquely qualified to write about the moor and its people.

Walking on Dartmoor, by John Earle. Published by Cicerone Press in 1987 and reprinted in 1990. More comprehensive than Starkey's books, and the author is not afraid of very long walks over remote parts of the moor.

Water from the Moor, by David J. Hawkins. Published by Devon Books in 1987. Useful and informative history of the use of Dartmoor as a water resource.

Finally, two very useful periodicals:–

Dartmoor Magazine. Published quarterly by Quay Publications (Brixham). Interesting and original articles on all aspects of the moor.

Dartmoor Visitor. Published annually in newspaper format by the Dartmoor National Park Authority and available from their Information Centres.

A last word on the subject of books. I bought and sold collectable books as a sideline for 3 years and came across many good books, but several with worn or torn dustwrappers which greatly reduced their value. It is so worthwhile to preserve the wrapper on a hardback book. I always cover the dustwrapper of a new book with folded polypropylene (not glued or taped) as soon as I take it home. Quite apart from preserving a book's financial value, it also maintains it in good condition as a work in itself, to be kept and valued and, hopefully, to outlive its owner.

A Head, 52, 53, 149
'A' Stone, 52, 53, 55
Abbots' Way, 18, 19, 40, 43, 44, 48, 49, 98, 111, 149
Adders, 10
Amicombe Brook, 30, 35, 125, 127
Amicombe Hill, 30, 34–35, 68, 70, 80, 81, 123, 125–128
Anderson, Rev. I. K., 35
Apple crusher (King Way), 65, 66
Arme (Erme) Head, 52
Aune Head Mire, 29, 70–76, 112, 114
Avon (Aune), River, 40, 43, 46, 71, 75, 93, 107, 108, 147
Avon Dam, 109
Avon Reservoir, 40, 111
Avon Valley, 40, 44, 73, 108, 111, 112, 115
Avon Waterworks, 108

Babeny, 97
Bagga Tor, 94
Baggator Brook, 97
Baggator Gate, 24, 26, 95
Bala Brook, 112, 114
Barnstaple, 28
Baskerville Hall, 41
Battyshull (Ryder's Hill), 46, 72
Batworthy, 101, 135, 143
Batworthy Brook, 101
Batworthy Corner, 101
Beardown Farm, 26
Beardown Man, 7, 93–99
Beardown Tor, 26, 79
Beast of Bodmin, 103
Beehive huts, 62
Bellever, 15, 97, 146, 147
Belstone, 122
Belstone Cleave, 120
Belstone Tor, 85, 118, 120, 121
Berrydown, 87
Birch Tor, 62, 104
Bittaford, 36, 38
Blachford, Manor of, 49
Black Down, 26
Black Hill, 28, 59, 116, 125, 140, 149
Black Lane (north), 95, 96
Black Lane (south), 59, 147–149
Black Ridge, 60, 125, 126, 149
Black Ridge Brook, 125
Black Tor (Avon), 108
Black Tor (West Okement), 80, 82, 126
Black-a-Tor Copse, 80, 127

Blackaton Brook, 130
Blackbrook, 16
Blacklane Brook, 53, 54
Blackmore, R. D., 85
Bleak House, 7, 34, 63–69, 123
Bodmin Moor, 55, 68, 103
Branscombe's Loaf, 69
Brentmoor House, 108
Bridestowe Station, 66
Broad Amicombe Hole, 82, 125–128
Broad Down, 56
Broad Falls, 112
Broad Marsh, 9, 57–58
Broad Mead, 55
Broad Rock, 49, 50, 52, 53, 55, 149
Brock, Mrs (Teignhead Farm), 85
Brown Heath, 40
Buckfast Abbey, 43
Buckfastleigh, 149
Buckland Abbey, 18
Buckland-in-the-Moor, 146, 147
Bunting, Snow, 104
Burrator Reservoir, 16, 55
Butterbrook, 38
Buttern, 134
Buttern Hill, 90
Buzzards, 56, 57, 104

Cantrell China Clay Drying Works, 36, 37, 39
Caters Beam, 16, 40, 149
Chagford, 85, 87, 101
Chagford Hydro-electric Station, 32
Chalk Ford, 22
Childe's Tomb, 19, 20
China clay, 37, 39, 40, 44
Cocks Hill, 98, 99
Coffin Wood, 97
Combe, 41
Combestone Tor, 71, 72, 76
Conan Doyle, Sir Arthur, 15, 23, 40, 89
Conies Down, 97
Conies Down Tor, 97
Conies Down Water, 97
Corn Ridge, 35, 63, 79, 80, 82, 83, 134
Corndon Tor, 146
Cornwood, 49
Cosdon Beacon, 46, 47, 107, 114, 118–120, 131
Cosdon Hill, see Cosdon Beacon
Cowsic Head, 70, 96
Cowsic, River, 16, 25, 94, 97
Cowsic Valley, 96, 97

Crane Hill, 16, 40, 70
Cranmere Pool, 7, 27, 56, 78, 83, 85–92, 116, 123, 149
Creaber, 90
Cross Furzes, 40
Crossing, William, 54, 85, 87, 103, 107, 114, 152
Crossways, 39, 44
Crow Tor, 24
Cuckoo, 59
Cut Combe Water, 25, 125
Cut Hill, 27, 28, 30, 58–60, 78, 116, 119, 140, 149
Cut Hill Stream, 58
Cut Lane, 148
Cut Lane Stream, 58

Dart, River, 46, 76, 147
Dart Valley, 30, 31, 72
Dartmeet, 41, 56
Dartmoor Letter Box 100 Club, 85–87
Dartmoor National Park, 77, 78, 139, 146, 151, 153
Dartmoor, birds on, 49, 56, 57, 59, 69, 75, 78, 104
Dartmoor, cattle on, 74, 103, 112–113
Dartmoor, industries on, 63, 69
Dartmoor, man on, 93, 99
Dartmoor, military activity on, 77–79
Dartmoor, ponies on, 103
Dartmoor, rainfall on, 147
Dartmoor, sheep on, 103–104
Dartmouth, 28
Devil's Tor, 26, 94, 96
Devon Stannary, 50
Devonport, 16
Devonport Leat, 16, 17, 23, 26, 48, 50, 55
Devonport Water Company, 50
Dinger Tor, 81, 83
Ditsworthy Warren, 43
Double Waters, 95
Dry Lake (upper Erme), 46, 76, 149
Dryework, 46
Dryfeldford, 46
Duchy of Cornwall, 44, 47
Ducks Pool, 18, 54, 85, 86
Dunnabridge Pound, 114
Dunnagoat Tors, 34, 67, 68

East Dart Head, 27, 28, 59
East Dart River, 28, 46, 56–58, 88, 91, 140, 147
East Dart Valley, 7, 56–62, 97, 146

East Mill Tor, 83
East Okement River, 47, 78, 147
East Webburn River, 146
Eastern Red Lake, 30, 95, 125
Eastern Whitebarrow, 44, 46, 107–115
Edward VIII, 87
Elephant's Nest Inn, 31
Elysburghe (Eylesbarrow), 47
Erme Head, 47, 52, 149
Erme Pits, 6, 18, 45–55, 114, 149
Erme, River, 21, 37, 40, 47, 50, 52–53, 80, 93, 147–148
Erme Valley, 30, 31, 40, 44, 55, 114
Ernestorre (Yes Tor), 47
Ester Whyteburghe (Eastern Whitebarrow), 46
Eylesbarrow, 9, 18, 47
Eylesbarrow Cairn, 54, 149
Eylesbarrow Mine, 54, 55

Fernworthy, 15, 140
Fernworthy Forest, 62, 101, 103, 114, 134, 135, 138, 142
Firing range information, 7
Fishlake Mire, 40, 73–75, 85
Flat Tor, 59
Foggintor Quarry, 146
Forder Brook, 134
Fordsland Ledge, 80, 84
Forest of Dartmoor, 18, 41, 43, 45–47, 49, 52, 54, 69, 72, 80, 95, 99, 100–101, 104, 106, 131
Fox Tor, 16, 20, 21, 59
Fox Tor Farm, 21
Fox Tor Gert, 21
Fox Tor Mire, 9, 15–23, 29, 40, 50, 55, 71, 75, 76, 120
Fur Tor, 7, 24–28, 30, 34, 36, 47, 59, 71, 81, 82, 85, 88, 96, 119, 123, 125, 126, 140
Fur Tor Brook, 26, 30, 125
Furnum Regis (King's Oven), 46

Gallaven (Gartaven) Ford, 133, 134
Gallaven Brook, 87, 133, 134
Gallaven Mire, 133
Gallaven Track, 130, 131
Ger Tor, 31, 35, 78, 129
Gidleigh, 87, 90
Gidleigh Common, 130
Goldsmith's Cross, 19
Goldsmith, Sir Malcolm, 19
Great Gnats Head, 49, 54, 55

Great Grimpen Mire, 15, 23, 40
Great Kneeset, 7, 25, 81, 119, 123–129
Great Links Tor, 26, 27, 66–68, 88, 114, 119, 127
Great Mire, 138
Great Mire Stream (Manga Brook), 138
Great Mis Tor, 8, 26, 47, 95, 111, 114, 148
Great Varracombe, 142
Great Western Railway, 37
Green Hill, 40, 73, 74, 93, 149
Green Hill Micas, 39
Green Tor, 34, 67–69, 148
Green Tor Water, 129
Gren Tor, 67, 69
Grey Wethers, 62, 93
Grims Grave, 55
Grippers Hill, 111
Grouse, Red, 49, 69, 75
Grymesgrove, 47, 52
Gutter Tor, 55

Hameldown, 111, 146
Hand Hill, 16, 19, 48, 49, 98
Hangingstone Hill, 27, 59, 88, 106, 116–119, 138–140
Hare Tor, 35, 68, 88, 123, 129
Harford Moor Gate, 38
Hartland Tor, 56, 57, 62
Hay Tor, 56, 146, 147
Hayford Hall, 40, 41
Headland Warren, 43
Headon, 133
Heath Stone, 46
Hcighestone (Longstone), 46
Hemerdon Ball, 77
Hemery, Eric, 133, 138, 142, 149, 151, 152
Hen Tor, 43
Henroost Tin Mine, 76
Henry III, 45
Hew (Hugh) Lake Foot, 46, 47, 104, 106, 114
Hew Lake, 104
Hexworthy, 71, 146
Hexworthy Mine, 114
Hickaton Hill, 40, 43
High Willhays, 26, 69, 83, 84, 88, 118, 119, 126
Higher Dunnagoat Tor, 67, 68
Highwayman Inn, Sourton, 63
Hillson's House, 30
Hobajons Cross, 38

Hoga de Cossdonne (Cosdon Hill), 46, 47
Holmes, Sherlock, 15
Holne, 41
Holne Moor Leat, 76
Holne Ridge, 71
Homerton Hill, 84
Honeybag Tor, 147
Hooper, John, 23
Hooten Wheals Tin Mine, 76
Horndon, 31
Hornfels, 79
Horns Cross, 71, 72
Horrabridge, 95
Horse Hole, 24
Hound of the Baskervilles, 15, 23, 40, 89, 152
Hound Tor (east), 56, 146
Hound Tor (north), 7, 46, 90, 106, 131, 133
Hunt Tor, 69
Hunters' Stone, 108
Huntingdon Clapper Bridge, 42, 43
Huntingdon Cross, 40, 42, 43
Huntingdon Warren, 40, 41, 43, 73, 111, 112
Hut circles, 93, 147

Isle of Wight, 73
Ivybridge, 121

Jobbers' Road, 43, 49, 111, 149
Joyner, Captain, 61

Keble Martin's Chapel, 43
Keble Martin, Rev. F., 43
Kennon Hill, 90, 131, 134
Kestor Rock, 101
King Way, 65, 66
King's Oven, 46
King's Tor, 146, 147
Kingsley, Charles, 85
Kistvaens, 55, 93, 147
Kit Hill, 140
Kit Rocks, 59
Kit Steps, 58
Kite, Red, 104
Kitty Tor, 35, 69, 127
Knack (Knock) Mine, 120

La Rede Lake (Red Lake), 46
La West Solle (Stenga Tor), 47
Lade Hill Brook, 57, 62
Lane Head, 31, 32, 123, 129

Langcombe Brook, 55
Langcombe Hill, 55, 70
Langestone (Heath Stone), 46
Langridge, 104
Laughter Tor, 146
Lee Moor, 37
Lee Moor China Clay Works, 37, 69
Leftlake Pit, 40
Letterboxes, 85–87
Lich Path (Way), 24, 97–99
Limsboro Cairn, 47, 95
Lints Tor, 7, 26, 77–84, 127
Lints Tor Brook, 81, 83
Little Hound Tor, 131
Little Kneeset, 35, 125
Little Varracombe, 60, 142
Logan stones, 67
London & South Western Railway, 63,
    66, 79
Longstone, 46, 94, 101, 135
Longstone Hill, 80, 84
Lower Dunnagoat Tor, 67, 68
Lud Gate, 40, 43
Lullingesfote (Limsboro Cairn), 47
Lyd Head, 35
Lyd, River, 66, 69, 147
Lydford, 97
Lydford Tor, 26
Lynch Tor 26, 47, 94, 95

Maish Hill Brook, 60
Manga Brook (Great Mire Stream), 138
Manga Farm, 61, 135, 143
Manga Hill, 104
Manga Hole, 134, 143–144
Manga Rock, 104
Maps, 13, 90
Mardle, River, 22
Mardle Valley Tin Mine, 22
Mary Tavy, 26, 31, 35
Mary Tavy Hydro-electric Station, 31–32
Meavy Aqueduct, 16
Meavy, River, 16, 17
Meldon Quarry, 63, 79
Meldon Reservoir, 35, 69, 79, 80, 84, 91
Merrivale, 95, 149
Merrivale Firing Range, 7, 24, 77, 94, 147
Merrivale Quarry, 69
Metheral Hill, 133
Mewyburghe (White Barrow), 47
Middle Brook, 114
Ministry of Defence, 78
Moortown, 130

Moute's Inn, 140
Mystor (Great Mis Tor), 47

Nakers Hill, 21, 40, 70, 74, 75, 112
Napoleon, 77
Narrator Brook, 16
Nat Tor, 32
Nattor Farm, 31
Newbridge, 147
Newleycombe Lake, 16
North Hessary Tor, 111, 114
North Teign River, 61, 104, 106, 114,
    118, 134, 135, 139, 140, 142, 143, 145
North West Passage, 60
Nun's (Siward's) Cross, 17, 18, 20, 47, 55
Nun's Cross Brook, 19,48
Nun's Cross Farm, 17, 18, 23, 40, 48, 55
Nun's Cross Ford, 98
Nun's Cross Hill, 16
Nun's Cross Tunnel, 16, 17

O Brook, 46, 76
Observation Post 15 (Okement Hill), 78,
    91, 116
Ockerton Court, 91, 92
Oke Tor, 116
Okebrokesfote (O Brook/Dart conflu-
    ence), 46
Okehampton, 87, 116
Okehampton Camp, 77, 90, 91
Okehampton Firing Range, 7, 24, 77, 79,
    84, 127, 147, 148
Okement Hill, 7, 27, 83, 90, 91, 116–122,
    127
Over Tor, 148

Parva Hunde Torre (Hound Tor), 46
Peat passes, 59–60, 147–148
Perambulation (of Forest), 18, 43, 45–47,
    52, 95
Perrott, James, 85, 92
Peter Tavy, 94
Petre's Bound Stone, 73
Petre's Cross, 113
Petre's Pit, 112
Petre, Sir William, 112
Petre-on-the-Mount, 73
Phillpott's Cave, 53
Phillpotts, Frank, 59, 60, 139, 147–148
Piles Copse, 80
Pillow mounds, 43, 112
Pinswell, 125
Plover, Golden, 78

Plym Ford, 9, 49, 54, 55
Plym Head, 18
Plym, River, 50, 93, 147
Plym Steps, 55
Plym Valley, 49, 98
Plymouth, 50
Plymouth Corporation Waterworks, 55
Plympton, 77
Plymstock, 19
Portland, 72
Postbridge, 56, 62, 91, 97
Princetown, 5, 15, 16, 23, 41, 48, 146, 147
Princetown railway, 69
Pupers Hill, 40

Quickbeam Hill, 40
Quinter's (Quintin's) Man, 135, 140–142

Rakernebrokysfote (Rattlebrook Foot), 47
Rattlebrook, 30, 34, 47, 67, 68, 128, 129
Rattlebrook Foot, 34, 47, 123, 124
Rattlebrook Head, 66, 69
Rattlebrook Hill, 68
Rattlebrook Peat Works, 66, 67
Rattlebrook Peat Works Railway, 66–68
Raybarrow Pool, 131
Red Lake, 36–44, 46, 47, 51, 52, 56, 73, 111, 112, 114
Red Lake China Clay Works, 36, 37, 40
Red Lake Tramway, 36, 37, 39, 114
Rival Tor, 90, 106, 134
Rough Tor, 24
Round Pound, 101
Roundy Park, 57
Ruelake Pit, 114
Ryder's Hill, 46, 71–73, 75, 111, 112
Ryder's Mire, 73
Ryder's Rings, 108

Sand Parks, 19
Sand Path, 139
Sandy Ford (Tavy), 30, 125, 126
Sandy Ford (West Okement), 80
Sandy Hole Pass, 57, 58
Sandy Road, 133
Sandy Way, 46
Scad, The, 129
Scorhill Circle, 87, 88, 93
Scorhill Down, 139
Scorhill Farm, 87
Sharp Tor (north), 68
Shavercombe Head, 55

Sheep tics, 12
Sheepfold, The, 114
Sheepstor, 149
Sheepstor Brook, 16, 55
Shelstone Tor, 134
Sheriff of Devon, 45
Shilstone Tor, 134
Shipley Bridge, 107, 112, 114
Shipley Bridge Naptha Works, 44, 68, 112, 113
Shipley Leat, 108
Shovel Down, 94, 101, 102, 135, 143
Sittaford Tor, 60, 61, 135
Siward's (Nun's) Cross, 17, 18, 20, 47, 55
Skir Gut (Gert), 76
Skir Hill, 76, 114
Snowdon, 111, 112
Sourton, 63, 64, 69
Sourton Common, 66
Sourton Ice Works, 65
Sourton Tors, 63–65
Soussons Warren, 43
South Downs , 72
South Hessary Tor, 16, 47
South Tawton, 131
South Zeal, 130
St. Boniface Down (Isle of Wight), 73
St. Michael of Halstock, Chapel of, 47
Stall Down, 30
Standing stones, 93
Standon Down, 94
Standon Hill, 32
Statts House, 59, 60
Steeperton Brook, 90, 119, 120, 133
Steeperton Gorge, 120, 121
Steeperton Tor, 88, 118–121, 133
Stenga Tor, 29, 47, 69, 80, 127
Stingers Hill, 37
Stone circles, 93, 147
Stone rows, 93, 94, 147
Stone Tor, 103, 104
Stone Tor Brook, 104
Strand Magazine, 23
Strane River, 22
Strolls, 65
Summer Brook, 24
Summer Hill, 24
Swincombe, River, 16, 17, 21, 22, 148

Tarka Trail, 78
Tavistock, 19, 43
Tavy Cleave, 7, 29–35, 68, 123, 129
Tavy Cleave Tors, 32, 33, 35

Tavy Head, 34, 70, 71, 96, 149
Tavy, River, 19, 25, 28, 30, 32, 35, 68, 80, 93, 95–97, 99, 123–126, 147
Tavy Valley, 32, 125
Taw Head, 78
Taw Marsh, 85, 120, 121
Taw, River, 28, 59, 78, 88, 90, 116, 120, 147
Taw Valley, 27, 120
Teign Head, 142
Teign, River, 46, 61, 72, 147
Teign-e-ver, 139
Teignhead clapper bridge, 135–136, 143
Teignhead Farm, 61, 85, 135, 137–138, 142, 143
Teignhead Newtake, 104, 134, 135, 142
Ten Tors Expedition, 28, 61
Ter Hill, 16, 21, 40, 113
Thirlstone (Thurlestone), 46, 105
Thornworthy Tor, 101
Three Barrows, 30
Throwleigh, 130, 131
Throwleigh Common, 130
Thurlestone Sands, 105
Tin mining, 50, 52
Trowlesworthy Warren, 43
Two Bridges, 25, 26, 80, 146
Two Bridges Hotel, 24

Varracombe Brook, 142
Vitifer Mine Leat, 61
Vitifer Tin Mine, 62
Vixen Tor, 15

Walkham Head, 95, 96, 149
Walkham Head Peat Works, 96
Walkham, River, 93, 95, 98, 99, 147
Walkham Valley, 96, 146, 148
Walkhampton, 18
Walking clothes, 10–12
Walking equipment, 13–14
Walla Brook (East Dart), 46
Walla Brook (North Teign), 87, 88, 106, 118, 134, 139
Wapsworthy Common, 94
Warrens, 43
Waterloo, 63
Watern Combe, 118, 139
Watern Oke, 34, 35, 125
Watern Tor, 7, 46, 87, 100–106, 134, 139
Watson, Dr., 15, 23

Weather forecasts, 9
West Dart Head, 59, 96
West Dart River, 16, 24–26, 46, 147
West Dart Valley, 80, 146
West Mill Tor, 83, 116, 118
West of England Compressed Peat Company, 68
West Okement River, 26, 80, 88, 89, 91, 92, 127, 134, 147
West Okement Valley, 29, 30, 31, 35, 69, 80–84, 91, 127, 128
West Webburn River, 146
Western Beacon, 38
Western Red Lake, 30, 95, 125
Western Wellabrook, 41, 43, 46, 111, 112
Western Whitebarrow, 44, 107–115
Wheal Betsy Tin Mine, 95
Wheal Emma Leat, 22, 76
Wheal Friendship Copper Mine, 31
Wheal Friendship Leat, 31, 32, 123
Wheal Jewel Reservoir, 32
Wheal Katherine Tin Mine, 9, 54
Whealam Stream, 19
White Barrow, 47, 95, 99
White Moor Circle, 131, 132
White Moor Stone, 131, 132
Whitehorse Hill, 7, 59, 85, 88, 118, 135–145
Whitemoor Marsh, 134
Whiteworks Mine, 6, 16, 18, 22, 23, 48, 50
Whittenknowles Rocks, 55
Widecombe, 56, 146
Wild Tor, 106, 118, 119
Wild Tor Well, 133
Willsworthy, 31
Willsworthy Firing Range, 7, 31, 77, 147
Winney's Down, 59
Wistman's Wood, 24, 80
Woodcock Hill, 35, 67
Wotesbrokelakesfote (Hew Lake Foot), 46, 47, 104

Yar Tor, 146
Yealm, River, 93, 147
Yes Tor, 26, 47, 65, 69, 79, 83–84, 118–119, 126
Ysfother (South Hessary Tor), 47

Zeal Gulley, 109
Zeal Tor Tramway, 112

✳✳✳✳✳

THE AUTHOR

Michael Hedges was born in Winchester in 1954 and now lives near Portsmouth with his wife, Jennifer, and three sons, Andrew, Ian and David. A chartered civil engineer by profession, he works in the water industry and, in his spare time, enjoys reading, watching sport and fulfilling a general interest in the rural landscape.

It was in 1982 that Michael first became acquainted with Dartmoor, when he felt a strong urge to recapture that sense of the unknown: this, he considered, could no longer be found in his native Hampshire countryside due to the encroachment of houses, roads and civilisation in general. Thereafter, he quickly developed a passion for exploring the moor by means of a succession of walks, often accompanied by his wife and, in latter years, by his three sons.

Dartmoor's main attraction so far as Michael is concerned is quite simply the fact that it is one of the few genuine wildernesses left in England. He has found, like many other people, that walking in its innermost depths provides a way of escaping from the pressures and routines of daily life. The vast Dartmoor landscape is deeply mysterious and unspoilt, and for him, walking on the moor is always accompanied by a sense of exploring the unknown.

The reason that Michael was moved to write this, his first, book was a desire to convey to others the fascination that this unique place holds for him and to inspire them to explore it for themselves. For those who know the moor already, he hopes that it will articulate their own feelings about walking in this timeless wilderness.

Michael Hedges